CULTURES OF THE WORLD

Saudi Arabia

Cavendish
Square

New York

Published in 2015 by Cavendish Square Publishing, LLC
243 5th Avenue, Suite 136, New York, NY 10016

Copyright © 2015 by Cavendish Square Publishing, LLC

First Edition

Website: cavendishsq.com

This publication represents the opinions and views of the author based on his or her personal experience, knowledge, and
research. The information in this book serves as a general guide only. The author and publisher have used their best efforts
in preparing this book and disclaim liability rising directly or indirectly from the use and application of this book.

CPSIA Compliance Information: Batch #WS14CSQ

All websites were available and accurate when this book was sent to press.

Library of Congress Cataloging-in-Publication Data

Janin, Hunt, 1940-
  Saudi Arabia / Hunt Janin, Margaret Besheer, Michael Spilling, Debbie Nevins.
    pages cm. — (Cultures of the world)
  Includes bibliographical references and index.
  ISBN 978-0-76144-996-6 (hardcover) ISBN 978-0-76147-996-3 (ebook)
  1. Saudi Arabia—Juvenile literature. I. Besheer, Margaret. II. Title.

  DS204.25.J362 2014
  953.8—dc23

                            2014008496

Writers: Hunt Janin, Margaret Besheer; Deborah Nevins—3rd ed.
Editorial Director Third Edition: Dean Miller
Editor Third Edition: Deborah Nevins
Art Director, Third Edition: Jeffrey Talbot
Designer Third Edition: Jessica Nevins
Production Manager: Jennifer Ryder-Talbot
Production Editors: Andrew Coddington and David McNamara
Picture researcher Third Edition: Jessica Nevins

Printed in the United States of America

CONTENTS

SAUDI ARABIA TODAY

THE KINGDOM OF SAUDI ARABIA IS A NEW COUNTRY IN A VERY old part of the world. The nation itself is less than a century old and in some ways is the creation of just one man. Even that one man, Abdul Aziz ibn Saud, probably could not have imagined what he was setting in motion when he fought for the mostly barren land that would become his kingdom.

Or perhaps he could. He named the country after himself, after all. And certainly he set out to father a large number of offspring, who would eventually produce the thousands of members of today's royal family, an entire social stratum unto themselves. But did he foresee the astonishing wealth the future held for his kingdom?

Thanks to the abundant oil discovered under its surface, Saudi Arabia today is one of the wealthiest countries on Earth, and in some ways, one of its most successful. It boasts gorgeous cosmopolitan cities, bustling ports, state-of-the-art industrial complexes, and modern hospitals offering free health care to all citizens. All this from a country that was, not so very long ago, a land of nomads, camels, and date palms. But even before it was Saudi, just merely Arabia, this country had something

The Royal Clock Tower in Mecca is the tallest clock tower in the world, and one of the tallest buildings.

that no other country has. Something the country treasures even more than oil.

It has Mecca. Mecca is the birthplace of Muhammad, the Prophet of Islam. That means Saudi Arabia is the birthplace of Islam itself. Fittingly, the religion is the bedrock of the country in virtually every way. A particularly conservative style of Islam dominates the culture. It is the basis of the law, the social structure, and the Kingdom's political worldview.

Saudi Arabia is the most male-dominated society in the world. Saudi women are restricted in ways that many people in Western countries find hard to accept. Until recently, Saudi Arabia was the last remaining country that denied women the right to vote. Beginning in 2015, thanks to reforms put in place by King Abdullah, women there will finally be allowed to vote. However, it's worth noting that citizens of the Kingdom, men and women alike, do not vote for their national leaders in any event. Saudi Arabia doesn't pretend to be a democracy. The ballot box exists for limited low-level municipal elections only.

The Kingdom is also the only nation that bans women from driving. In addition, the country's strict guardianship system also prevents women from opening bank accounts, working, traveling, and going to school without the express permission of their male guardian. Just as the king has the final say in the matters of the nation, a Saudi man generally has the final say in matters of the family, and especially regarding the women in his family.

The entire society is designed to keep the sexes segregated. Men and women do not mix socially, work together, or pray together. They do not travel on public transportation together. Men board a bus through the front entrance; women must enter in the back. At wedding receptions, the sexes party in separate rooms. In public, all women must cloak themselves to prevent an unrelated man from seeing her face, hair, and body.

This system of extreme segregation is justified by the strict interpretation of Islam that the state adheres to. Many other Muslim nations take a less rigid view. The restrictions can cause women awkward difficulties in day-to-day life. For example, a woman might take her children to one of the glittering shopping malls for a fun afternoon. She can treat them to ice cream cones in the food court—little girls don't have to cover themselves—but if she wishes to enjoy one as well, the experience becomes quite a challenge. The full body cloak covers the mouth.

Far more important, though, the gender segregation can be life threatening. In 2002, for example, a fire broke out at a girl's school in Mecca.

For Saudi women, even small pleasures, such as eating in public, can be a challenge.

As the girls fled in terror, the religious police would not allow them to escape and actually chased them back into the burning school to get their headscarves and abayas, the black robes that women must wear in public. More than fifteen girls died. Even the state-owned Saudi media was horrified at that event. More recently, in 2014, a young university student in Riyadh died of a heart attack when male paramedics were prevented from entering the women's-only campus for two hours.

At a McDonald's restaurant in Riyadh, a segregation board separates male and female customers. All restaurants in Saudi Arabia are divided into the family section and the men's section.

As Saudi Arabia progresses through the twenty-first century, reforms seem certain. And there is evidence that the current regime recognizes that some change may be necessary. The country needs to do business with the rest of the world, and in this age of Facebook, Twitter, YouTube, and the like—which Saudi women have access to—the world is watching. In 2009, King Abdullah named Norah al-Fayez, a U.S.-educated former teacher, as the first female minister in the government. She became deputy education minister in charge of women's education. And in 2014, Somayya Jabarti became the first woman editor-in-chief of a newspaper, the English language *Saudi Gazette*.

As part of the nationwide "Saudization" campaign to produce more homegrown professionals, the country is encouraging young women and men alike to study internationally. These younger, educated Saudis are vocal in discussions about their country's future. The country must figure out how to balance its ancient cultural and religious traditions with the demands and expectations of the modern world.

Meanwhile, the country faces other issues as well. Some are the same problems facing Americans in the twenty-first century. Heart disease and stroke, for example, top the list of causes of early death in Saudi Arabia, as they do in other industrialized countries. Saudis will need to examine their lifestyles, with attention to diet and exercise, to improve their health.

Other concerns are specific to the Saudis' position in the world, both geographically and politically. Finding enough water to support a growing population in this dry country is one of the most important challenges. Maintaining stability in the midst of one of the world's most volatile regions will be another.

Two little boys join the men in prayer on the morning of a religious holiday.

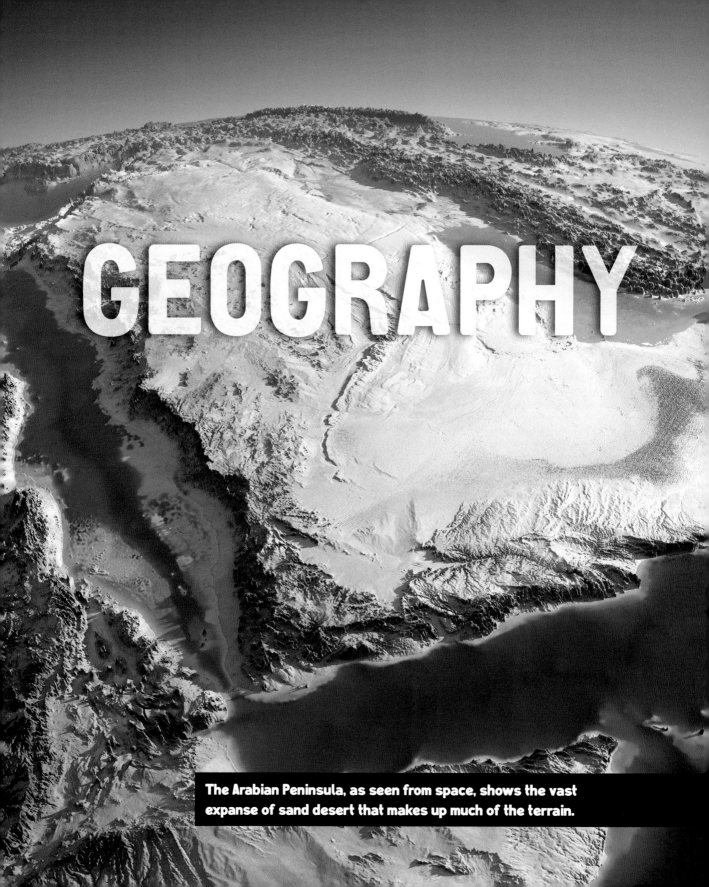

GEOGRAPHY

The Arabian Peninsula, as seen from space, shows the vast expanse of sand desert that makes up much of the terrain.

1

SAUDI ARABIA IS A BIG COUNTRY. IT is located on the Arabian Peninsula, a vast chunk of boot-shaped land that bridges the continents of Asia and Africa. Although the peninsula is geographically situated in the far western part of Asia, this part of the world is often called the Near East or Middle East, terms that originated from the European point of view.

Saudi Arabia is the largest country in the world without a river.

The luxurious Kingdom Centre building in Riyadh is a landmark of Saudi Arabia's capital city.

Saudi Arabia occupies four-fifths of the Arabian Peninsula, with an area of 865,000 square miles (2,240,350 square km), which is nearly a quarter the size of the United States. Saudi Arabia borders Jordan, Iraq, and Kuwait to the north, Yemen and Oman to the south, and the Persian Gulf, Qatar, and the United Arab Emirates to the east. It is separated from Egypt, Sudan, and Eritrea by the Red Sea in the west.

Unique rock formations in the desert mark the famous Al-Hasa Caves in southeastern Saudi Arabia.

Seen in its geographical entirety, Saudi Arabia is a huge, tilted plateau that rises sharply from the Red Sea in the west and then slopes gradually down to the Persian Gulf in the east. It is a land of extremes. The interior of the country contains many sharp mountain ridges and great areas of sand. Saudi Arabian mountains rise to more than 9,000 feet (2,743 m) and can be freezing cold in winter. They tower above sand or gravel deserts where summer temperatures often exceed 120°F (49°C) and where it rarely rains. There are no lakes, no permanent rivers, no big forests—Saudi Arabia is probably the driest large country on the face of the Earth. It is not an easy or a soft land, but it does have an austere beauty of its own.

GEOLOGICAL HISTORY

Africa and the Arabian Peninsula were once fused together. About 70 million years ago, heat and stresses within the earth caused this land mass to split at the rift line now marked by the Red Sea. The Arabian part moved to the northeast. The Red Sea edge of the peninsula rose sharply, forming the western Hijaz Mountains; the rest of the peninsula sloped east toward the Persian Gulf. Later, fiery lava fields covered much of the tilted Hijaz.

The low eastern areas under water received sedimentary deposits. This explains why oil is found chiefly in Al-Hasa or under the waters of the Gulf. Oil comes from the billions of tiny plants and animals that died millions of years ago, raining down upon the sea floor to form sedimentary beds.

THE FOUR MAIN REGIONS

Saudi Arabia contains four main geographic regions: the Najd, Hijaz, Al-Hasa, and Asir.

NAJD With an average elevation of 2,000 to 3,000 feet (610 to 914 m) above sea level, the Najd is a vast eroded plateau located in the central heartland of Saudi Arabia. Much of the Najd is desert: the Nafud Desert in the north, ad-Dahna in the east, and part of the immense Rubal-Khali in the south.

The Najd is the traditional home of the ruling Saud family. Saudi Arabia's bustling capital, Riyadh, once a sleepy mud-walled village, is located here. The nomads of the Najd are known for their generosity, bravery, and love of poetry.

HIJAZ The Hijaz has the greatest variety of people, ranging from desert Arabs to the descendants of Africans. It is the most geographically diverse region and lies in the west, in the range of mountains running parallel to the Red Sea coast. The Hijaz contains the narrow coastal strip known as the Tihamah, where the port of Jeddah is located. More importantly, the Hijaz contains the two holiest cities of Islam: Mecca and Medina.

AL-HASA Al-Hasa embraces the flat eastern coast of Saudi Arabia along the Persian Gulf. This region has lush oases, where farmers tend vividly green gardens in the midst of the desert. Most of Saudi Arabia's oil is found here, as

All the oil of the Gulf states—Iran, Iraq, Saudi Arabia, Kuwait, Bahrain, Qatar, and the United Arab Emirates—comes from the same geological formation known as the Arabian Platform. Together, these countries contain more than half of the world's proven oil reserves.

The Rub al-Khali, known as the Empty Quarter, is in the southeastern corner of Saudi Arabia. It is the greatest continuous expanse of sand in the world. About the size of the state of Texas, it covers approximately 264,000 square miles (683,760 square km)— roughly one-third of the entire country. Virtually uninhabited and subjected to blistering heat in summer days and below-freezing temperatures in winter nights, the Empty Quarter is one of the driest and most desolate places on Earth.

Some of the sand in this gigantic desert stays put, but much of it is blown about into curving dunes by the incessant, ever-shifting winds. Seen from above, a typical sand dune assumes a U shape, like a huge horseshoe. Some of these sand dunes can reach a height of 330 feet (100 m).

are the great oil cities of Dhahran and Dammam. Much of Saudi Arabia's oil is shipped to world consumers by tankers loaded at Ras Tanura on the Gulf. Al-Hasa has a population of more than 908,000—most of them Shia Muslims.

ASIR Mountainous Asir is in the southwestern corner of Saudi Arabia near neighboring Yemen. Because its relatively generous rainfall made terraced agriculture possible, Asir was known to the ancient Romans as *Arabia Felix*, meaning "happy" or "flourishing" Arabia. Asir's major city is Abha, perched at an elevation of around 8,000 feet (2,428 m).

CLIMATE

Saudi Arabia's climate differs from one part of the country to another. It has a generally dry climate, with high temperatures in summer in most areas and particularly high temperatures in the central and northern areas. In the south, however, the temperature is normally moderate, dropping on the Sarawat Mountains in Asir to as low as 50°F (10°C) in summer. In winter, temperatures generally become moderate, turning cold at night, when it sometimes drops to below freezing, especially on the western mountains and along the northern borders.

Because of climatic patterns, rain-bringing weather usually bypasses the Arabian Peninsula. Rainfall in most parts of Saudi Arabia is therefore uneven and unreliable. On the average, less than 4 inches (10 cm) of rain falls on Jeddah, Riyadh, or Dhahran each year. But this figure masks big regional variations.

The real pattern is usually one of drought or cloudburst. Along the Red Sea coast, torrential rains can fall in March and April. The highlands of Asir can get more than 20 inches (51 cm) of monsoon rain per year. At the other extreme, however, a desert can go without any rain at all for ten consecutive

Saudi children walk through a flooded street in the Red Sea port city of Jeddah following a heavy rain.

An oasis is a fertile place in a sand or gravel desert. Providing a green contrast to its dry surroundings, it is a welcome sight to weary, thirsty travelers. Some oases consist merely of a few palm trees around a spring or well. Others cover vast areas, like the Al-Hasa oasis, which is supplied by water from more than fifty artesian springs. Covering 70 square miles (182 square km), Al-Hasa includes the towns of Hofuf and Mubarraz and many villages supporting a vast permanent population. Tamarisk trees on the borders of the oasis help keep desert sand from spreading over the carefully tended gardens, which produce lush fruit, vegetables, and grains. Dates, citrus fruit, melons, tomatoes, onions, rice, wheat, barley, and henna (a plant used to make a reddish dye that women use to decorate their hands and feet and men use to tint their beards) are grown here.

years. Still, when rain does come to this parched land, the results are magical: seeds hidden dormant in the earth for years suddenly bloom in a matter of hours, and the apparently lifeless desert turns green for a few days.

FLORA

Except for parts of rainy Asir, where wild olives and some larger trees grow, and the scattered oases where date palms are cultivated, there are few true trees in Saudi Arabia. The types of plants that have adapted to the harsh environment are all hardy, drought-resistant, and stunted. Most of them are brown or greenish-brown, except after infrequent rains, when patches of green herbs and colorful flowers can quickly bloom and wither. Often hundreds of consecutive square miles of the country can be covered by drought-adapted species such as the rimth saltbush or the yellow-flowered arfai. In some parts, small tamarisk and acacia trees are common.

Saudi Arabia's flora may be limited, but what is available is quite unusual. The frankincense tree, for example, produces a dried resin that used to be extremely costly. Large amounts of frankincense were burned in the religious celebrations of the ancient Middle East to perfume ceremonies and sacrifices. One shrub, known as the "toothbrush bush," is used by nomads to clean their teeth. Herbs of the desert are also used to season and preserve food, to perfume clothes, and for washing hair.

The tough, fierce honey badger is a native of the Arabian Peninsula, much of Africa, and Southwest Asia.

FAUNA

Wildlife of Saudi Arabia include the wolf, jackal, hyena, and baboon. Among the smaller animals are the fox, hedgehog, Arabian hare, jerboa (kangaroo rat), and ratel (honey badger). The gazelle, ibex, leopard, and other larger mammals were once common throughout most of Arabia, but their numbers were diminished by overhunting in the 1930s.

Since 1986, however, Saudi Arabia's National Commission for Wildlife Conservation has set aside eight reserves to protect threatened animals and plants. The first of these to be set up was a 5,237-square mile (13,564-square km) reserve near Ta'if, not far from Jeddah. This reserve is a protected zone for endangered gazelles and the reintroduced oryx that became extinct in the wild in the early 1960s.

Birds are a common sight in the Kingdom. Large numbers of flamingos, storks, swallows, and other birds cross the Arabian Peninsula during their annual migrations. Some winter in Saudi Arabia. Native birds include sand grouse, larks, bustards, quails, eagles, and buzzards. Gulls, pelicans, and other water birds live along the coasts.

Many species of snakes, lizards, and scorpions abound in the desert region. Domesticated animals include the camel (the chief support of nomadic life in the desert), horse, sheep, goat, and donkey.

CITIES OF THE KINGDOM

The major urban areas of Saudi Arabia are Riyadh, the capital, located in the interior; Jeddah, a key port and commercial center on the Red Sea; the Dhahran/Dammam/Al Khobar complex, the center of oil production, near the Gulf coast; and Mecca and Medina, the two holiest cities of Islam, located in the western hills of the Hijaz.

RIYADH When Abdul Aziz, founder of the Kingdom of Saudi Arabia, captured Riyadh in a camel raid in 1902, it was a tiny mud-brick village in the wilderness of central Arabia. It remained something of a backwater until the sharp run-up of oil prices after 1973 turned it into a boom town. The Saudis then wanted to modernize their capital. They succeeded so well that Riyadh has grown more quickly than any other city in the Middle East. In less than fifty years, Riyadh was transformed from a mud-walled town of 25,000 inhabitants into an international metropolis of more than five million people.

Today Riyadh is a sprawling urban city highlighted by a combination of modernist and traditional Arab architecture. Many modern conveniences are readily available, as is air conditioning. Reflecting Riyadh's importance as a world capital, the entire diplomatic corps moved there from Jeddah in the 1980s. There are now ninety-three embassies and other diplomatic missions in Riyadh, all located in a separate diplomatic enclave near the city. The city is served by the King Khalid International Airport, which was opened in 1983. Since 2002 the capacity of the airport has doubled to accommodate fifteen million passengers, and soon expects to be able to handle thirty-five million.

THE CORAL GARDEN OF THE RED SEA

Saudi Arabia's seas offer unparalleled panoramas of underwater life. The brilliantly colored marine life of the long and narrow Red Sea—about 1,150 miles (1,851 km) long and 180 miles (290 km) wide—is a spectacular example of Saudi Arabia's natural beauty.

The clear, warm, shallow areas of this body of water provide the perfect environment for the growth of corals, which come in a wide range of sizes, shapes, and colors. Their names suggest their rich diversity: there are hard, soft, black, fire (these can sting divers badly), brain (shaped like a giant human brain), mushroom, bushy, and fan corals. Seen under water, these formations are so abundant and so beautiful that they are often referred to as "coral gardens."

To swim over the crest of a Red Sea reef while wearing a face mask and to look down at the bottom through 30 feet (55 m) of clear, warm, sunlit water is to see an unforgettable, colorful profusion of marine life. Among the harmless and most brightly colored fish in the coral gardens are parrotfish, butterfly fish, pennant fish, royal angelfish, and coral trout. Some less common and more dangerous creatures include lionfish, stonefish, stingrays, moray eels, and sharks.

JEDDAH Traditionally known as the "Bride of the Red Sea," Jeddah is an ancient commercial port that handled much of the spice trade of the Red Sea and served as the gateway for pilgrims coming to nearby Mecca. Like Riyadh, Jeddah also grew explosively during the oil boom. The old harbor, which had become a bottleneck for the entry of badly needed building materials and

The beautiful Corniche Mosque is just one of the attractions in Jeddah.

consumer items, was rebuilt into a modern port capable of handling 22.6 million tons (2 billion kg) of freight each year. A new airport covering forty square miles (104 square km)—the King Abdul Aziz International Airport—was constructed to ease the entry into the Kingdom of more than 1.5 million Muslim pilgrims each year. The population of Jeddah is now about 2.5 million people. Many residents think their city is more charming than Riyadh, even if it lacks the capital's political and financial importance.

DHAHRAN/DAMMAM/AL KHOBAR This port-city complex consisting of Dhahran, Dammam, and Al Khobar has also experienced rapid growth in recent years. It is the home of Saudi Aramco, an oil company, and of the University of Petroleum and Minerals. The three oil cities, with a population of about 900,000, serve as an outlet to the world for the vast petroleum-gathering and petrochemical industries of the Al-Hasa region. King Fahd International Airport serves this booming region.

MECCA Formerly a market town for camel caravans, Mecca is the birthplace of Islam. Throughout its history, Mecca has been venerated as a holy place and has attracted Arabs from every part of the Arabian Peninsula, as well as Muslims from around the world. When the annual tide of *hajj* (HAHJ) pilgrims floods in, Mecca's population temporarily approaches two million. Normally, however, the city is much smaller, with a population of about 1.5 million. Mecca contains the Grand Mosque, where the great *Ka'bah* (kah-AH-bah), the holiest shrine of Islam and the focal point of Islamic worship, is located.

MEDINA After Mecca, Medina is the second most important city for Muslims. It is where Prophet Muhammad, Islam's founder, took refuge from the persecution taking place in Mecca. Medina's most venerated historic site is Muhammad's tomb, located in the Prophet's mosque. Medina also houses an Islamic University and the famous King Abdul Aziz Library, which contains a huge collection of some 564,000 books on religious topics, as well as a collection of rare copies of the Qur'an, some in the form of manuscripts written hundreds of years ago. Medina has a population of about one million.

INTERNET LINKS

www.islamiclandmarks.com
Islamic Landmarks has slide shows and videos of important locations throughout the Arab world. (Note that the city of Mecca is spelled *Makkah* on this site.)

www.arriyadh.com/eng
Riyadh City website has day-to-day information aimed at residents of the city.

www.jeddah.gov.sa/english
The official website of the Jeddah Municipality. It contains information about the city and slide shows.

HISTORY

The clay and mud-brick Masmak Fort in Riyadh is where Abdul Aziz Ibn Saud captured the city in 1902. Today it is a museum.

2

S AUDI ARABIA, FOUNDED IN 1932, has been a country for less than a century. But civilization has existed here since ancient times. The earliest human presence in the Arabian Peninsula dates back some 15,000 to 20,000 years, and by 1000 BCE, a lively civilization was well developed in certain regions. Ancient Saudi history is relatively difficult to find from an archaeological perspective, partly because the desert sand has buried much of the country's ancient treasures. The defining event for the establishment of today's culture, however, was the birth of the Prophet Muhammad, the founder of Islam in 571 CE.

Saudi Arabia has two UNESCO World Heritage sites:
· Madain Saleh, a 2,000-year-old site of pre-Islamic caves and tombs
· The At-Turaif District in ad-Dir'iyah, the first capital of the Saudi Dynasty, founded in the fifteenth century

THE EARLIEST PEOPLE

In prehistoric times, Stone Age hunter-gatherers drifted out of eastern Africa into the Arabian Peninsula, which was then lush and well-watered. About 15,000 years ago, however, the weather grew warmer,

Stone tombs in the desert date back 5,000 years.

deserts began to spread, and the rivers disappeared. Some of the inhabitants became nomads herding camels, goats, and sheep. Others settled in small villages around oases or along the sea coasts and supported themselves by agriculture and trade.

Wedged between three major continents, the Arabian Peninsula was an important passage for caravans of traders crisscrossing the vast deserts, carrying frankincense and myrrh, silk and spices, gold, precious stones, and ivory to Egypt, Palestine, Syria, and ancient Babylon. Many of the early inhabitants of Arabia performed the important role of middlemen in this commercial link.

One group, called the Nabateans, settled in the northwestern part of Arabia, where they built a stronghold at Madain Saleh to control this trade. In 106 CE, however, the Romans captured the capital at Petra to strengthen their own hold on the trade routes of Arabia. This military conquest marked the beginning of the end of the Nabatean civilization.

Arabia continued to be a commercial crossroads, but infighting among the Arab groups for control of the trade routes resulted in instability. This eventually led to a general decline in trade and business. By 200 CE, parts of northern Saudi Arabia had been incorporated into the Roman province of Arabia. In the fourth and sixth centuries, southwestern Arabia fell under Abyssinian (Ethiopian) rule. Throughout all these years Arabia remained politically fragmented. By the beginning of the sixth century, it was still a collection of small warring states.

THE COMING OF THE PROPHET

The most important event, and turning point, in the history of the Arabian Peninsula was the birth of the Prophet Muhammad, the founder of Islam, in 571 CE. When the Prophet was born, his home town of Mecca was already a sacred place of worship of gods from an earlier religion.

Within his lifespan Muhammad established a new religion and laid the foundations of the Arab Empire. Preaching the oneness of Allah, he became the temporal and spiritual leader, as the Islamic faith substituted traditional tribal loyalties for the religious bond. A century later, Arabs, carrying the message of Islam, rode out of Arabia and conquered neighboring civilizations.

Mecca, where Muhammad was born, was a trading center for the camel caravans bringing goods along the Red Sea coast. Muhammad's parents died when he was young. Until age eight, he was raised by his grandfather. At the death of his grandfather, Muhammad's guardian was his uncle Abu Talib.

Muhammad himself was poor, but his prospects rose when, at about age twenty five, he married a rich widow fifteen years his senior. Although he was a good trader, Muhammad also had a strong religious inclination. When he reached his forties, he would retreat to a cave outside Mecca to pray and meditate on ways to improve the morality of his society. Tradition says it was there that the archangel Gabriel revealed to him the word of God.

Muhammad's first convert was his wife Khadija. By about 613 CE, he was publicly preaching about what had been revealed to him. His followers wrote down what he said and in so doing gradually compiled a holy book, the Qur'an (sometimes spelled Koran), which they believed had been dictated to Muhammad by God. Other Meccans, however, strenuously objected to his teachings because they might interfere with the spirit worship at the Ka'bah, and thus hurt Mecca financially. The Ka'bah was an ancient temple in Mecca, a pilgrimage center and sanctuary, and a destination for many nomads who came to worship their various tribal gods and spirits. To escape persecution, Muhammad and some of his followers moved in 622 to a neighboring city, first known as Yathrib and later as Medina. This emigration now marks the starting point of the Muslim calendar.

Muhammad's talents helped him to advance into a commanding military and political position in Medina. In 630, his forces conquered Mecca, where he transformed the Ka'bah into a shrine for Muslims. He treated the vanquished Meccans with dignity and honor. Most of them soon became followers of Islam. When Muhammad died in 632, he had founded what was shortly to become a new world religion.

ISLAM REACHES NEW LANDS

By the time Muhammad died in 632, the unification of the Arabian Peninsula was underway. Later, under the Umayyad dynasty (661—750), which ruled from Damascus, Islam spread rapidly, eventually reaching west into Spain and North Africa, north into Syria and Mesopotamia, and east into Afghanistan and parts of India.

Financial problems and feuding among Arab tribes weakened this dynasty, and it was soon overthrown. In its place arose the Abbasid dynasty (750—1258), which ruled from Baghdad (in today's Iraq) and made it the capital city. Baghdad soon became a world center of wealth and military power between the ninth and eleventh centuries, reaching a peak of glory under the rule of the fifth caliph, Harun al-Rashid, and his son. However, a gradual economic decline set in, sealing the fate of the Abbasids. In 1258 the Mongols sacked Baghdad: the last caliph was executed, and the streets of the city were piled high with corpses.

The Mamluks were a military caste that ruled Egypt from 1250 to 1517. During the fourteenth and fifteenth centuries they also controlled the Hijaz, including Mecca, Medina, and Jeddah. In 1517, however, the Ottoman sultan, Selim I from Turkey, conquered Egypt and assumed control of the Hijaz. His successor, Suleiman the Magnificent, spent huge amounts of money on fabulous new buildings for the holy cities of Islam.

THE RISE OF WAHHAB AND SAUD

In time, the Ottoman Empire weakened. Two important figures arose in the Najd, the heartland of the nomads. The first was an eighteenth-century Muslim preacher, Muhammad bin Abdul Wahhab. He wanted to purify Islam and rid it of the local customs and mystical influences that in his view had tainted it badly.

The second was a local sheikh of the Najd, Muhammad bin Saud, who wanted to protect and expand the territory his people controlled. The ambitions of these two men dovetailed nicely, and around about 1750 they decided to join forces.

The sons of Muhammad bin Saud and Muhammad bin Abdul Wahhab continued the ambitious plan of expansion their fathers had begun. By 1804 they had taken control of the holy cities of Mecca and Medina and had

The ruins of the old city of Dariyah, outside of Riyadh, date to the fifteenth century.

established a political-religious state embracing almost one million square miles (2.6 million square km) of the Arabian Peninsula.

Their success prompted the Ottoman Empire to send forces to retake the region. The Ottoman army recaptured the holy cities and, in 1818, had also captured the ancestral home of the Saud family in the Najd. Thus the House of Saud's first effort to found a kingdom ended in a dismal failure.

A second effort began in 1820 but it, too, failed. This time it was because a rival family, the Rashid dynasty, eventually seized Riyadh from Saud control in 1891 and forced the Saud family to flee to neighboring Kuwait. There the family waited for the opportunity to regain its lost lands.

THE FATHER OF SAUDI ARABIA

This chance finally came in 1902 when Abdul Aziz Ibn Saud (also known as Ibn Saud, son of Saud) led forty companions into the desert and, in a daring camel-back raid, captured Riyadh after fierce hand-to-hand fighting.

Abdul Aziz Ibn Saud was a very tall, physically powerful, and intelligent leader. He was a devout Muslim and spent part of each day in prayer and religious reading. To win the allegiance of the scattered, independent desert groups, he briefly married and then divorced (strictly in keeping with the customs of Islam—by not having more than four wives at a time) a very large number of women.

Abdul Aziz himself claimed that he had married more than 282 women and had fathered more than forty-six sons and many daughters. By the time of his death it was clear he had fathered at least fifty-eight officially recorded sons and an unrecorded number of daughters. These offspring form the core of today's huge royal family.

THE UNIFICATION OF SAUDI ARABIA

After capturing Riyadh, Abdul Aziz spent the next decade fighting the Rashid dynasty, which had the support of the Ottomans. He did not meet with much success. He finally decided to try to unite the nomads and encourage them to settle down. This he did by creating a religious brotherhood, which he called the *Ikhwan* (ik-WAHN), or "brethren." The Ikhwan spread the puritanical Wahhabi gospel favored by most of the nomads.

In 1914, backed by Ikhwan fighters, Abdul Aziz captured most of central Arabia and the Eastern Province and pushed the Ottomans from the Gulf coastline. At this time, however, the western region, the Hijaz, was under the rule of another rival, Hussein. Enlisting the help of the British adventurer and soldier T. E. Lawrence, Hussein defeated the Ottomans at Aqaba and proclaimed himself king of the Hijaz. The conflict between Hussein and Abdul Aziz for supremacy was inevitable. In 1925, after years of fighting, Abdul Aziz conquered the Hijaz region. In 1932 he unified Al-Hasa, the Najd, and the Hijaz into a new country known as the Kingdom of Saudi Arabia.

King Faisal ruled from 1964 until his assassination in 1975.

THE DEVELOPMENT OF A MODERN STATE

Saudi Arabia's stability owes much to the fact that a single dynasty has governed since Abdul Aziz Ibn Saud established the Kingdom in 1932. This was further enhanced by the discovery of oil in 1938, as oil wealth made it possible for King Abdul Aziz to begin the country's transformation into a modern state.

Saud, the eldest son of Abdul Aziz, became king when his father died in 1953. In 1964 King Saud abdicated in favor of his brother, Faisal, who ruled until his assassination in 1975. Faisal's rule saw the implementation of a program that started Saudi Arabia's drive toward modernization. Faisal was succeeded as king by his half-brother, Khalid. Economic development

U.S. Secretary of State Hillary Clinton meets with Saudi Foreign Minister Prince Saud Al Faisal in Washington D.C. in 2010.

continued rapidly, thanks to the rise of oil prices. More significantly, King Khalid's reign set in motion the Second Development Plan, which brought further improvements in the people's economic and social standards of living.

When King Khalid died in 1982, his brother Fahd became the fourth king and reigned until his death in 2005. His half brother Abdullah then became king. Abdullah, like Fahd, was one of the many sons of Ibn Saud. Already more than ninety years old, it's unlikey he will remain king much longer. More change seems to be certain in the coming years.

FOREIGN POLICY

Saudi Arabia has traditionally been on very good terms with Western countries, especially the United States. During the Cold War, Saudi Arabia had no formal relations with the Soviet Union, as it opposed the beliefs of communism.

Saudi Arabia has become an important mediator of regional conflicts. One of its most important foreign policy goals is to see a peaceful resolution to the conflict between the Palestinians and the Israelis. In March 2002, at a meeting of the Arab League, Crown Prince Abdullah put forth a plan for separate Israeli and Palestinian states to peacefully coexist. Saudi Arabia continues to play an active role in seeking a realistic resolution of the enmity between the two peoples.

In more recent years, Saudi Arabia has struggled to stay on good terms with the United States. It has opposed the Assad regime of Syria, and there has long been a deep rift between the Saudi Kingdom and both Iraq and Iran. On the other hand, the Kingdom has tried to build close relations with

Since inheriting the throne in 2005, King Abdullah has taken some bold steps. In 2009, he reshuffled his government with the aim of balancing the country's strict Islamic traditions with the needs of a modern economy. Many in the West view Saudi Arabia as one of the world's most backward countries, in terms of social and political issues. At the same time, it's the world's top producer of petroleum products and needs to function as a forward-looking country.

Abdullah fired several controversial officials, including the very strict chief of the religious police. The king put a more moderate cleric in charge. Abdullah also appointed the country's first female minister, in the department of women's education. In 2011, the king announced that women would have the right to vote in municipal elections starting in 2015, and in 2014, he appointed thirty women to the formerly all-male Shura Council.

Also under Abdullah's rule, Saudi Arabia lifted its ban on allowing women to compete in the Olympic Games. For the first time, two female athletes from Saudi Arabia participated in the London Summer Games in 2012.

While many people around the world see these reforms as small steps in the right direction, conservative clerics in Saudi Arabia have been angrily opposed to these changes. Abdullah has a difficult job bridging East and West, old and new— doing business with the international community while also protecting the power of the monarchy and ultra-traditional religion and culture.

the six members of the Gulf Cooperation Council (GCC), a political and economic alliance founded in 1981 that includes Saudi Arabia, Kuwait, the United Arab Emirates, Qatar, Bahrain and Oman. The group's purpose is to unite its member nations on the basis of their similar political and cultural identities, which are rooted in Islamic beliefs.

THE GULF WARS

Saudi soldiers examine debris from an Iraqi Scud missile that landed in downtown Riyadh in 1991, during the first Gulf War.

During the 1990 conflict in the Gulf, in which the ground fighting itself lasted only 100 hours, more than 600,000 troops from thirty-seven countries were deployed to Saudi Arabia.

Iraq's unprovoked attack on its neighbor, Kuwait, in August 1990, posed a dilemma for Saudi Arabia. Both the Saudis and the Americans feared that Iraq would try to capture the oil fields in the eastern part of the Kingdom.

The Saudis recognized that they did not have the military power needed to stop an invasion by Iraq. King Fahd decided that the wisest course of action was to join forces with the Americans and their allies in hopes of defeating Iraq as quickly as possible.

Five days after the Iraqi attack on Kuwait, U.S. troops began to arrive in Saudi Arabia. In November 1990, the United Nations Security Council authorized the use of "all necessary means" to expel Iraq from Kuwait. When Iraq failed to withdraw, the Gulf War began in January 1991. The war cost the Saudi government an estimated $37.5 billion. Without Saudi Arabia's full military and financial cooperation, the United States and its allies might not have won the war so quickly.

On the other hand, when the United States invaded Iraq in 2003, Saudi Arabia was not a supportive ally. Although it wanted to maintain good relations with the United States, and did not support the regime of Saddam Hussein in Iraq, the Saudi kingdom did not support this war effort. It did not allow U.S. forces to use Saudi land as staging grounds for attacks on Iraq.

TERRORISM IN THE TWENTY-FIRST CENTURY

Terrorism has become a fact of life in the twenty-first century. Every country has been affected by it or the threat of it. People from more than sixty nations were killed in the attacks on the World Trade Center in New York on September 11, 2001.

Saudi Arabia feels the sting of terrorism particularly strongly. Fifteen of the nineteen hijackers aboard the airliners that crashed in New York, Virginia, and Pennsylvania in 2001 were Saudi citizens. Because of this, the Kingdom has been criticized for not having done enough to stop religious fervor from growing within its borders.

Osama bin Laden, the leader of the al-Qaeda terrorist network and the man behind the September 11 attacks, was originally a Saudi citizen. He was born into the extremely wealthy bin Laden family, but rejected the privileges of his upbringing. He left his homeland to pursue *jihad*. Broadly defined, *jihad* means "to struggle in the way of Allah." It can be interpreted to mean, nonviolently, "the inner struggle to fulfill one's religious duties." However, it can also be interpreted to mean "to struggle against those who do not

Two American soldiers walk through a Safeway store in Al-Khobar in 1990. Some Saudis objected to having U.S. troops stationed in Saudi Arabia.

U.S. and Saudi investigators gather evidence following the terrorist bombing of the Khobar Towers in 1996.

believe in Allah" and even "to engage in armed struggle against persecution and oppression." Because of his beliefs, as well as his continued outspoken criticism of the Saudi King Fahd, the Kingdom stripped him of his Saudi citizenship in 1994. U.S. forces killed bin Laden in Pakistan in 2011.

Saudi Arabia has also been the victim of terrorism on its shores. In 1996 an apartment building complex in eastern Saudi Arabia housing U.S. military personnel was attacked by a truck carrying explosives. Nineteen Americans were killed at the Khobar Towers. Saudi Arabia worked hard in cooperation with the United States to bring the perpetrators to justice.

The Kingdom strongly condemns acts of terrorism, saying that they are forbidden by Islam. The government actively pursues an anti-terrorism policy and works with the United States and the international community in the war on terrorism. Nevertheless, rumors maintain that terrorist training camps operate within its borders, and that the government supports terrorist groups outside of its borders.

SAUDI - AMERICAN RELATIONS AFTER SEPTEMBER 11, 2001

To say that Saudi Arabia's relationship with the United States was strained after the Sept. 11, 2001 terrorist attacks is an understatement. Fifteen of the nineteen airline hijackers were Saudi nationals, as was Osama bin Laden, the mastermind behind the attacks. The American public became highly suspicious of the Kingdom and of President George W. Bush's personal relationship with the Saud royal family, which had been close.

On the other side, many influential clerics in Saudi Arabia spread anti-Americanism and urged Muslims to take militant actions against the United States. One of their strongest complaints was that the United States had troops stationed in Saudi Arabia, and most objectionably of all, in the holy cities of Mecca and Medina. Indeed, that fact was one of the major reasons given for the September 11 attacks by bin Laden.

The U.S. Congress accused Saudi Arabia of secretly financing terrorist groups, which the Kingdom denied. Nevertheless, suspicion remains. In 2003, the United States withdrew its troops from Saudi Arabia. Though they don't agree on many things, both countries recognize their mutual need for the other. Their relations are strained, but not broken.

INTERNET LINKS

www.saudiembassy.net/about/country-information/history.aspx
The site of the Royal Embassy of Saudi Arabia in Washington, D.C. has good sections about Saudi history and many other topics.

www.bbc.com/news/world-middle-east-14703523
BBC News Middle East Saudi Arabia Profile
A quick timeline of events in the nation's history.

www.pbs.org/wgbh/pages/frontline/shows/saudi/
PBS Frontline: *Saudi Time Bomb?*
This companion site to the 2001 TV show has the transcript plus other features including interviews and an in-depth timeline.

GOVERNMENT

The Arabic script at the center of the green and white Saudi Arabian flag says, "There is no god but God; Muhammad is the Messenger of God."

3

SAUDI ARABIA IS AN ABSOLUTE monarchy, meaning the king has absolute legal power. The king heads the government, and is also the prime minister, the president of the Council of Ministers, and the commander-in-chief of the armed forces. His official title is the "Custodian of the Two Holy Mosques," meaning the mosques of Mecca and Medina, and he is also the head of the royal House of Saud. The king combines in his person all the major functions of government—executive, legislative, and judicial.

Saudi Arabia's first written constitution was adopted in 1992 under King Fahd. The constitution confirms the monarchy as the nation's system of government, and Islamic law as the foundation of government. This body of law, called *sharia* (SHAH-ree-ah), is based on the Qur'an and the example of the prophet Muhammad, and has been refined through the centuries by Muslim legal scholars. Strict adherence to sharia law is ensured by the Muslim *ulema* (oo-ley-MAH). They are Wahhabi clerics (clergymen of a particularly strict branch of Islam) who advise the king on the application of sharia law in various matters—from law-making to the punishment of offenses.

Since 1953, when the nation's founding king Abdul Aziz Ibn Saud died, the Saudi throne has passed on to five of his many sons. When there are no more direct heirs of that generation, the throne will pass to his sons' sons, and then their sons, and so on.

The Saudi Shura, or Consulative Council, is the closest thing the kingdom has to a parliament.

NATIONAL AND LOCAL GOVERNMENT

The king appoints a Council of Ministers, which has numerous legislative, executive, and administrative duties and a considerable say in what goes on at the national and local level. The king, however, can veto the Council's decisions and can replace its ministers at will.

The Consultative Council was inaugurated on December 29, 1993. It consists of appointed members, shares authority with the government, and advises the Council of Ministers. The members are chosen from the academic, business, and religious elite. Besides reviewing laws and government policies, the Consultative Council is empowered to recommend that the king reject those laws or policies found lacking. But the king has the final word in state affairs.

Setting up the Consultative Council meant broadening the participation of Saudi citizens in their own governments. No longer would the Saudi royal princes have a monopoly on decision-making. The number of members in the Consultative Council has increased from its initial sixty to 150 members.

For administrative purposes, Saudi Arabia is divided into thirteen provinces. Each province has a governor, who is often a senior-ranking prince of the al-Saud family, as well as a deputy governor. The provincial governors are appointed by the King.

Each province has a council consisting of officials and private citizens. They are appointed, not elected. It is the job of the provincial councils to study local issues and present reports to the Minister of the Interior in Riyadh, who then acts on the reports as he sees fit.

Despite this apparent decentralization, however, in practice Saudi Arabia is run very much from the top down—all the important decisions are made in Riyadh. There are no self-sufficient elected local governments, as there are in the United States, at the city and state level.

In the Kingdom of Saudi Arabia, all the local administrative units depend entirely on the capital for policy guidance and for financial support. Riyadh, in turn, assumes full responsibility for supporting the provincial councils.

Apart from the election of some low-level advisors to help the chief municipal executives, there are no elections in Saudi Arabia. Furthermore, since Saudi Arabia is a monarchy, there are no political parties.

HOW DECISIONS ARE MADE

Decisions at all levels in Saudi Arabia—national, local, tribal, or family—are made only after an informal, usually lengthy, discussion and consultation. One goal is to make sure that all views are heard, not only so that good ideas will surface, but also to give everybody a chance to participate personally and have a say in the decision-making process.

A man casts his vote at a polling station in 2005. The municipal election was the kingdom's first-ever election, open to male voters only.

The building of the Ministry of Internal Security in Riyadh exhibits impressive architectural design.

Personal participation is most noticeable in the daily *majlis* (MAHJ-lis), or public audience held by high officials. Each day, for example, Prince Khalid bin Bandar Al Saud, the governor of Riyadh, reads petitions presented to him in person by a long line of supplicants. He then passes the petitions on to an aide for appropriate action.

One of the king's most important responsibilities is to find enough common ground among the different elements in the society so that a consensus can eventually be reached. Maintaining this kind of public forum in an increasingly complex society is quite challenging. Sometimes a consensus cannot be found, and the final decision must be made and imposed from above. In other words, the king has the final say and his decision is absolute.

KEEPING THE PEACE

Given the frequent wars in the Middle East, Saudi Arabia is lucky. It has been blessed with relative peace and stability ever since it was formally created in

1932. It has never been invaded by another country. There has been one attempted insurrection, in 1979, when a radical fundamentalist and nearly five hundred of his well-armed followers seized the Grand Mosque in Mecca. They accused the Saudi government of allowing Western influences to contaminate Saudi culture and Islam. They held thousands of worshippers hostage in the huge compound. The siege lasted two weeks and took hundreds of lives before the militants were captured and executed.

Saudi children celebrate as King Abdullah arrives in the capital in 2011 after spending three months abroad. A poster of the king is in the background.

Saudi Arabia's special relationship with the United States, coupled with its own armed forces, has helped to keep the peace. In addition, the Saudis have spent billions of their oil dollars on defense, investing in a highly sophisticated air defense network and buying a great deal of other advanced weaponry from the West.

INTERNET LINKS

www.saudiembassy.net/about/country-information/government
The Royal Embassy of Saudi Arabia in Washington D.C. offers a broad selection of information from a pro-Saudi perspective.

www.saudi.gov.sa/wps/portal/yesserRoot/aboutKingdom/rulingSystem
This official Saudi government site offers a basic overview of the government.

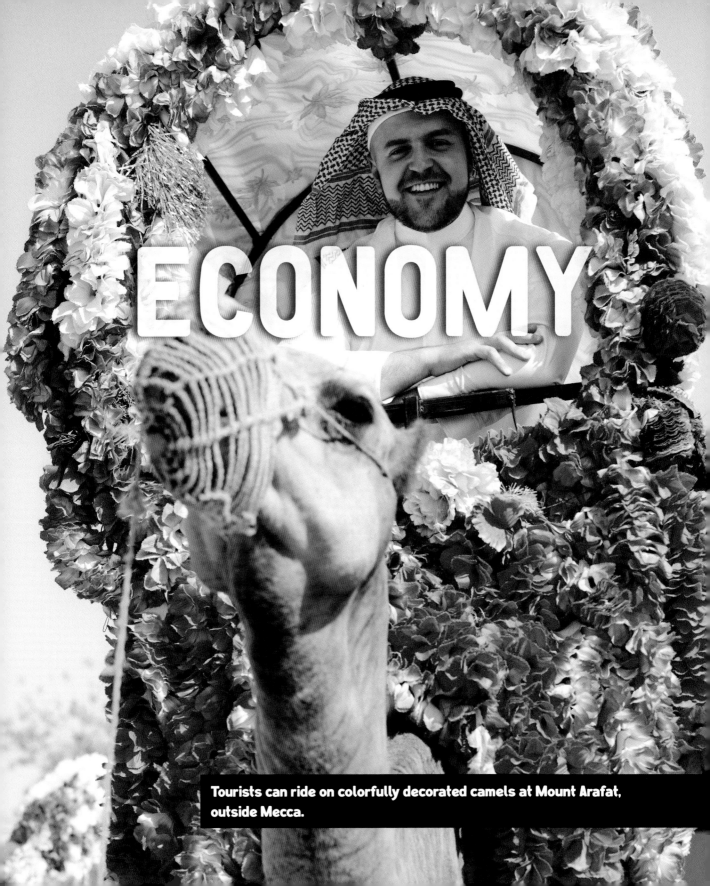

ECONOMY

Tourists can ride on colorfully decorated camels at Mount Arafat, outside Mecca.

4

SAUDI ARABIA DID NOT START OUT AS a wealthy country. Its economy, such as it was, consisted of subsistence agriculture, services for pilgrims traveling to holy sites, and regional date plantations. The discovery of oil in the Eastern Province in 1938, when the nation was a mere six years old, changed everything.

More than 95 percent of all Saudi oil is produced by the state-owned Saudi Arabian Oil Company (Saudi Aramco). It is the world's largest oil company.

The quantity and variety of dates in the market speak to the importance of the fruit to the Saudi diet and economy.

Oil would completely transform Saudi Arabia into a modern nation. At the same time, the West's growing demand for oil spurred the speedy development of the Kingdom's oil industry. Wealth began flowing into the country as quickly as oil flowed out of it. The economy boomed again in the 1970s, when oil prices rose rapidly. In short, Saudi Arabia blossomed from a remote desert land into an international powerhouse.

The Kingdom's revenue from the sale of its oil has allowed Saudi Arabia to design and finance ambitious development projects that have set world records for size and cost.

The full extent of Saudi Arabia's petroleum resources is still not known: oil companies keep finding more oil and gas. But it is thought that Saudi Arabia has roughly 17 percent of the world's proven reserves of crude oil and its gas reserves are the fifth-largest in the world.

Affiliates of the Saudi government's General Petroleum and Minerals Organization (Petromin) handle oil refining, as well as the production and marketing of refined petroleum products. Since Saudi Arabia has few other resources and is the world's leading oil exporter, petroleum is still the

The deputy interior ministers of the six nations that make up the Gulf Cooperation Council meet in 2013 in Riyadh.

BLACK GOLD: THE MANY USES OF PETROLEUM

Petroleum (crude oil) is a thick, dark liquid that will burn and produce energy when heated to very high temperatures. Petroleum consists of a mixture of complicated chemical compounds known as hydrocarbons. When oil is heated, these hydrocarbons are released. Different types of hydrocarbon combinations determine which of many products are produced, but all are useful for the functioning of modern society.

When petroleum is heated, nearly half of what is refined becomes gasoline. Gasoline is used to power everything from cars to lawn mowers and small airplanes. Another product is diesel fuel, used in the engines of trucks, ships, and trains. Fuel oils are used for heating homes and buildings, as well as powering ships and industrial plants. Kerosene is used to power jet engines and tractors. Tar and asphalt are also by-products of this process. They are used for making roads.

These are not all the uses of "black gold." Refining also produces petrochemicals— chemical compounds from the hydrocarbons of petroleum. Both natural gas and refinery by-products are used to make petrochemicals, which in turn are transformed into a variety of end products, such as plastics, artificial rubber, synthetic fibers for clothing, fertilizers for farms, additives for food, high explosives, dyes, cosmetics, paint, ink, solvents, resins, and drugs.

mainspring of the economy. It contributes two-thirds of the government's revenues and 90 percent of the country's export earnings.

Saudi Arabia's production of crude oil and the value of that oil vary considerably from year to year. It depends on the economic forces of supply and demand, as well as other very complicated factors. Oil prices can be quite volatile, meaning they go up and down in response to many things, and are hard to predict. Sometimes, there is too much oil on the world market and prices tumble. This may be good news for consumers (it means that gasoline and other forms of oil-based energy will be cheaper), but it spells trouble for oil producers because their income falls. When this happens, plans to develop the country may have to be shelved.

The Organization of Petroleum-Exporting Countries (OPEC) was founded in 1960 by Saudi Arabia and other major oil exporters for the purpose of

An oil pump in the desert taps into Saudi Arabia's vast underground sea of petroleum.

trying to stabilize oil supply and price. But the cycle of boom-and-bust continues because oil prices are pegged to world events. When such events happen, OPEC stabilizes oil prices by increasing or reducing oil output. In July 2008, oil prices reached a new high of $147 per barrel. But a worldwide economic crisis a few months later caused the price to plummet to below $35 per barrel by the end of that year. Recent political unrest in the Middle East has driven the price up again.

FINDING AND PUMPING OIL

When searching for oil, the first thing to look for is a geologic *petroleum trap*. This is an underground rock formation that prevents the petroleum from rising to the surface and causes it to accumulate in a reservoir.

In Saudi Arabia, geologists often use sound waves, which are generated by small explosions, to look for traps. Sound waves bounce off rocks hidden deep in the ground. Some of these impulses are reflected back to the surface and are recorded on a sensitive instrument known as a seismograph. Although a seismograph cannot show whether there is any oil in a particular formation, it does give an accurate picture of geological structure. Geologists can then estimate the probability of oil being found in that area and drilling can begin.

Wells can also be drilled offshore in the Persian Gulf, either from special ships or by three-legged "jackups" that rest on the bottom of the sea. Because there is so much oil under eastern Saudi Arabia and the Gulf, finding oil in this region is easier than it would be in other parts of the world.

No matter where the oil is found, the next step is to get it out of the ground. Oil in the earth is under natural pressure. If the pressure is high enough, it will flow up the well to the surface without any assistance. When the pressure is very high, it can produce a dramatic gusher, which must be capped and brought under control so that the oil and gas forced up into the air will not go to waste. The Saudis are especially lucky: not only do they have

WHERE DOES THE WATER COME FROM?

Saudi Arabia may be oil rich, but it is water poor. For a big country with no rivers or lakes and very little rainfall, however, it still manages to support a population of millions of thirsty people, a number of major cities, a huge petroleum industry, and a fair amount of agriculture. Where does this desert country find its precious water? The answer is, to some extent, in the same place it found its other treasure—underground.

Deep in bedrock of the Arabian Peninsula are vast underground reservoirs of water called aquifers. After locating and mapping these resources in the 1970s, the Saudi government drilled many thousands of wells to tap the water. In the beginning, the aquifers held enough water to fill Lake Erie. But they are not replenished by rain, like above-ground lakes, and several decades of draining them have greatly reduced their size. To find more sources of water, the Saudis had only to look to the seas on their eastern and west coasts.

Of course, seawater is not potable, or drinkable, as it is. Therefore, the government has invested in desalinating facilities that remove salt from the seawater. Saudi Arabia is the world's foremost producer of desalinated water. Seventy percent of the water for the cities comes from these facilities. Desalinated water also supplies industry and the generation of electrical power.

A water tower in Riyadh

Other water resources include the recycling of water for use in irrigation, and the capture of surface water from annual runoff and flash floods in the mountains. Saudi Arabia has worked hard to salvage every drop it can. Nevertheless, the country could be facing a water crisis. Finding enough water to support this rapidly growing country will continue to be one of the government's top priorities in the years to come.

the world's biggest oil field—the Ghawar field, which is around 150 miles (242 km) long and 20 miles (32 km) at its widest—but their oil is also under enough natural pressure to flow readily without much pumping. This makes it cheap to produce.

PIPELINES AND SHIPS

Oil pipes from Saudi Arabia pass through Bahrain in the Middle East.

Once the oil has been brought to the surface, it must be moved to world markets. This is done by pipelines and ships. Local pipelines in eastern Saudi Arabia gather crude oil or gas from the Ghawar and other fields and deliver it to the petroleum-handling port of Ras Tanura. Oil tankers then take it out to other ports with refineries. Some oil is refined in the Kingdom itself, but it has usually been more economical for the Saudis to ship the crude oil elsewhere to be refined.

The most important pipeline, from a strategic point of view, is the Petroline system, which carries oil and gas from the eastern fields of Saudi Arabia all the way across the country to the petrochemicals facility and port of Yanbu on the Red Sea, 750 miles (1,207 km) to the west. The advantage of this route is that it avoids a bottleneck in the narrow Strait of Hormuz at the mouth of the Persian Gulf, which might be mined or otherwise closed in the event of war, thus preventing the export of Saudi petroleum. Yanbu offers not only security but also efficiency: large amounts of oil can be stored there safely, tankers can be loaded quickly, and a state-of-the-art computerized control room oversees the port's complex operations.

In the past refineries had to be built near oil fields because of the high cost of transportation, and not near the urban areas that actually paid for and used gasoline and other fuels. Big tankers, however, lowered shipping costs appreciably. Although Saudi Arabia has eight domestic refineries (and more in development) and produces about twelve million barrels of petroleum products per day, it also ships crude oil to be refined in other countries. Through joint business ventures, Saudi Arabia refines oil in the United States, South Korea, the Philippines, Greece, India, and China.

DEVELOPING THE DESERT

The oil boom of the 1970s gave Saudis the money and the reason to build an ultramodern economy in the desert. It built new cities, airports, ports,

'SAUDIZATION' AND THE PROBLEM OF FOREIGN WORKERS

Some five to seven million foreigners work in Saudi Arabia, and are called expatriates, *or expats for short. They come from countries such as Yemen, the Philippines, Sri Lanka, Egypt, Pakistan, and India. Many also come from Western Europe and the United States. In general, low-status workers, such as maids and manual laborers, come from poorer countries in South Asia. These workers are needed because upper- and even middle-class Saudis consider manual labor to be beneath them and refuse to do it.*

Higher-status workers, such as technology professionals, teachers, and nurses, come from the more industrialized countries. Traditionally these workers were necessary because Saudis did not have the education or technical expertise to work in certain industries, such as petrochemicals or aviation. However, reliance on foreign manpower is declining; thousands of Saudis graduate from the Kingdom's numerous universities and technical or vocational schools each year. Others are returning graduates and professionals from foreign institutions. Programs offered by local institutions form the backbone of the "Saudization" of the labor force. That is a campaign promoted by the Saudi government to decrease reliance on foreign manpower and to explore other sources of national income. However, the Saudization of the workforce does not extend to the lower-status jobs.

hospitals, schools, roads, and communication facilities.

The new industrial city of Jubail gives an idea of the speed and scale of the modernization process. Located on the Persian Gulf coast of Saudi Arabia, Jubail is the biggest public works project in modern history. Construction began in 1976, and eventually more than 50,000 workers were brought in from about sixty different countries. Jubail's cooling system brings seawater by canal from the gulf to cool the industrial machinery. The cooling system is the largest in the world.

King Khalid International Airport at Riyadh was opened in 1983, and covers an area of 225 square miles (583 square km). The beautiful Hajj Terminal at King Abdul Aziz Airport in Jeddah, opened in 1981, was inspired by the sweeping lines of Bedouin tents. With its gigantic roof covering 0.6 square miles (1.5 square km), it is the main entry point for pilgrims coming to Mecca on the hajj each year.

Circular fields of irrigated crops dot the otherwise barren landscape near Khouris.

Congestion at the port of Jeddah once forced ships to wait for weeks to unload. This led to delays in construction projects because supplies and equipment were held up in the port. But Jeddah, too, has been modernized and now has fifty-eight of Saudi Arabia's best piers. Yanbu, also on the Red Sea, has been developed to handle oil and petrochemical exports.

AGRICULTURE AND OTHER SECTORS OF THE ECONOMY

The government of Saudi Arabia has realized that its oil and gas reserves are not infinite. These resources will eventually dwindle, and alternative sources of energy may become cheaper. If so, the Kingdom will have to fall back on a more diversified, or varied, economy if it is to maintain a high standard of living.

At the same time, Saudis themselves must be trained to do much of the work now done by foreigners. For these reasons, Saudi Arabia has been investing heavily in other sectors of the economy—such as mining, aviation, agriculture, fishing, and manufacturing—and is teaching Saudi citizens how to work in these sectors.

This diversification can be quite dramatic. Seen from the air, the big green circular wheat fields near Riyadh are an unexpected sight. They are the result of modern automated pivot-centered irrigation systems that are more than half a mile in diameter and that successfully produce high-quality wheat. Thanks to the high prices offered by the Saudi government, farmers in the country can now grow more than double the amount of wheat their country needs. The excess is exported to other Gulf countries.

Saudi Arabia also exports a variety of fruit, such as watermelons and grapes. With sufficient water and abundant sunlight, much of the country's light windblown soil can be cultivated.

THE SWEETEST FRUIT OF THE OASIS

In Ash Sharqiyah (Eastern Province) lies Al-Hasa, the world's largest oasis. Millions of tall, lush palm trees have stood here for thousands of years. Hanging from the lower palm fronds are giant clusters of dates. More than 300 varieties of this fruit grow in Saudi Arabia.

Before oil was discovered in the 1930s, dates were Saudi Arabia's main export. Today, the Kingdom is the world's second-largest producer, supplying nearly 15 percent of the world market, in addition to sending dates as food aid to poorer parts of the world.

The date palm is a revered symbol in Saudi culture. Its importance is evident in the national emblem: a date palm suspended over two crossed swords. The date palm represents vitality and growth, while the swords represent justice and strength.

INTERNET LINKS

www.saudiaramco.com/en/home.html
Official site of the world's largest oil company.

www.english.globalarabnetwork.com/arab-world-news/saudi
English language site of the Global Arab Network has a page for Saudi articles, many related to economy.

ENVIRONMENT

A cormorant in the oily surf at Khafji, in northern Saudi Arabia, is a victim of a deliberate Iraqi oil spill into the Persian Gulf during the first Gulf War.

5

WATER, WATER, WATER—FINDING it, purifying it, conserving it— is by far Saudi Arabia's top environmental challenge. Nevertheless, like any country, it has other ecological issues to deal with as well. Water and coastal pollution from oil spills, carbon emissions from its production of petroleum products, other forms of air pollution, waste management, endangered species, and climate change are all pressing matters.

Scientists warn that climate change will increase temperatures and decrease rainfall in some areas of the country, while creating more extreme flooding in others. The government is aware of these issues and is working on them to be sure. However, the Saudi culture is not yet fully onboard with the concept of "green" living. Environmental awareness is not a big part of the Saudi consciousness in the public or business sectors. Recycling has not caught on in any significant way, and sewage problems and industrial spills are not uncommon.

Saudi Arabia's combination of vast deserts, rugged mountains, and green oases presents environmentalists with many challenges. The Kingdom has established several organizations, such as the National Commission for Wildlife Conservation and Development, for the purpose of protecting and preserving the country's ecosystem.

CONSERVATION EFFORTS

Saudi Arabia is a highly industrialized country, where limiting and containing pollution is a high priority. In the 1970s the government established regulations to limit harmful emissions. In 1981, it established the Meteorology and Environmental Protection Administration (MEPA) to improve the efficiency of national conservation efforts. One of MEPA's main tasks is to collect scientific data on the Kingdom's plant and animal species. This information provides a valuable basis for long-term environmental planning decisions, which are used especially by the industrial and defense sectors of the economy.

MEPA also monitors marine, land, and air pollution. Scientists regularly collect air, water, and soil samples from across the Kingdom to check for changes in the levels of organic and man-made pollutants. Monitoring such changes is very important for the long-term health of the people, plants, and animals of Saudi Arabia.

In 2001, the government went further, enacting the General Environmental Law. And in 2012, the Kingdom issued another nine environmental laws, establishing higher standards for air, water, chemical, and waste management.

A flare stack burns off excess gas at an oil refinery in the desert.

OIL SPILLS

Since Saudi Arabia is the world's largest producer of petroleum and petroleum products, taking special precaution to prevent oil spills is especially important. Tanker ships carrying crude and refined oil have double hulls to help prevent leaks and spills. However, accidents do occasionally occur, causing oil spills that can severely damage marine life.

During the Gulf War in 1991, the Iraqi regime deliberately caused a massive oil spill in the Persian Gulf by releasing eleven million gallons of crude oil into its waters as they retreated from Kuwait, Saudi Arabia's northern neighbor.

More than 800 miles of the Saudi and Kuwaiti coastline were affected by the oil. Contingency plans prepared by Saudi authorities helped to contain the environmental damage to the coastline, and as a result minimized the loss of marine life.

DESERTIFICATION

Much of Saudi Arabia is covered in sand; in fact, the world's largest sand desert—*Rub al-Khali* (The Empty Quarter)—stretches across the southern part of the country. The total annual rainfall in Riyadh averages 4 inches (10 cm), and there are no permanent rivers anywhere in the country.

This combination of dry weather and sand, coupled with the effects of climate change, poses a real environmental threat to Saudi Arabia's cities and agriculture. The problem is known as desertification. At Riyadh's King Saud University, students and scientists at the Center for Desert Studies work to

Irrigation creates productive farmland in the desert.

In 1989, the NCWCD, now called the Saudi Wildlife Commission, reintroduced animals that had become extinct in certain regions back into their original habitats. At the Mahazat Al-Sayd Reserve in southwestern Saudi Arabia, one of the fifteen reserves established and cared for by the commission, breeders reintroduced the wild Arabian oryx, *a type of white antelope, which had vanished from the wild in 1972.*

Scientists started new herds using some animals from a royal family member's private collection in Saudi Arabia and some from a breeding program at the Phoenix Zoo in the United States. Despite the highest hopes and best intentions, the program was not completely successful. Rainfall in some years was insufficient to sustain the herds, and fences around the reserves prevented the animals from roaming in search of vegetation. Also, poaching continues to be a problem. However, the effort to save the oryx goes on.

devise viable ways to keep drifting sands from encroaching into the cities. Some options for containing deserts include planting special plants, building fences, and using other means to stabilize or anchor the sand. The university dedicates much of its research to learning about the uniqueness of the desert environment. It uses that knowledge to develop programs to protect both the desert and the ecosystem that relies on it for survival. Such efforts aim to ensure the comfort of people's lives in the nearby cities.

SCIENTIFIC RESEARCH

The King Abdulaziz City for Science and Technology (KACST) functions as both the Saudi Arabian national science agency and its national laboratories. Each year, KACST awards millions of dollars in grants to scientists working

on a variety of projects in the Kingdom—in the fields of energy, agriculture, astronomy, aeronautics, the environment, and computer technology. Since its establishment in 1978, KACST has been the driving force behind Saudi Arabia's technological development.

CONSERVATION

Saudi Arabia's heritage is deeply embedded in the idea of living in harmony with nature. Out of this nomadic heritage, the Saudis have developed a great respect and affection for the fragility of nature. They are raised to believe that it is their social responsibility to care for and protect all endangered species from organic and man-made threats. Furthermore, Islam teaches that all living things are created with value and purpose and that it is the responsibility of human beings to conserve and protect the natural environment.

In 1986, the government established the National Commission for Wildlife Conservation and Development (NCWCD) for this purpose. Fifteen natural wildlife reserves, covering 2.5 percent of the total country, have been set aside for endangered plants and animals, protecting them from hunters and poachers. These areas extend to the Red Sea and the Persian Gulf. Another important conservation effort is the restoration of mangroves that have been damaged or are deteriorating.

INTERNET LINKS

www.kacst.edu.sa/en
The English language site of the King Abdulaziz City for Science and Technology (KACST) offers many pages of information about its goals and activities.

nwrc.gov.sa/NWRC_ENG
National Wildlife Research Center
This English-language site has photo galleries, slide shows, videos, and information.

SAUDI ARABIANS

A typical Saudi family goes for a walk in town.

6

ETHNICALLY, AS WELL AS nationally, the Saudi Arabian people are Arabs. That's perhaps stating the obvious, but the question may be asked: Who is an Arab? At its founding in 1946, The Arab League, an organization of Arab states, answered the question this way: "An Arab is a person whose language is Arabic, who lives in an Arabic speaking country, who is in sympathy with the aspirations of the Arabic speaking peoples."

Scholars consult texts in a library in the holy city of Medina.

"All that is best in the Arabs has come to them from the desert: their deep religious instinct, which has found expression in Islam; their sense of fellowship, which binds them as members of one faith; their pride of race; their generosity and sense of hospitality; their dignity and the regard which they have for the dignity of others as fellow human beings; their humor, their courage and patience; the language which they speak, and their passionate love of poetry."

–Sir Wilfred Thesiger, in *Arabian Sands* (1959)

Many Saudi Arabians are direct descendants of the ancient nomads, whose name has come down through the ages as *Aribi* or *Arabu* and who are now known as Arabs. The early Arabs lived in the northern deserts of the Arabian Peninsula. Some of them settled near oases and others remained nomadic.

A HOMOGENEOUS SOCIETY

The isolation of desert life kept the ancestral Arabs from mingling and mixing with other peoples, with the result that many Saudis are considered to be "pure" Arabs. One sign of this is that they are very similar physically and presumably resemble their nomadic ancestors. The rigors of desert living honed an Arab culture that is embodied in the Bedouin people. Pride in this Arab Bedouin heritage and its legendary generosity and kinship, in addition to their role as guardians of the holy cities of Mecca and Medina, give modern Saudis the confidence to be leaders in the Islamic world.

A woman carries her baby in an impoverished section of Riyadh.

DIVERSITY AT THE EDGES

Some racial and ethnic mixing did, however, occur along the fringes of the Arabian Peninsula. On the Red Sea coast, for example, some of the foreign pilgrims who came to Mecca from many parts of the world for the hajj stayed there and were absorbed into the indigenous population. Africans also migrated to this region. Therefore, in Jeddah today, there are Saudis with African backgrounds. Similarly, far to the east, migrants from Iran and India also settled down on the Persian Gulf coast and married the local people. Some Saudis in the Al-Hasa region today reflect this Persian and South Asian influence. Nonetheless, unlike the United States and some other countries, Saudi Arabia has never been a real melting pot of different cultures and peoples. While there more than five million foreigners working in the Kingdom, they are not considered part of Saudi society.

In 2013, the population was estimated to be around 26.9 million people

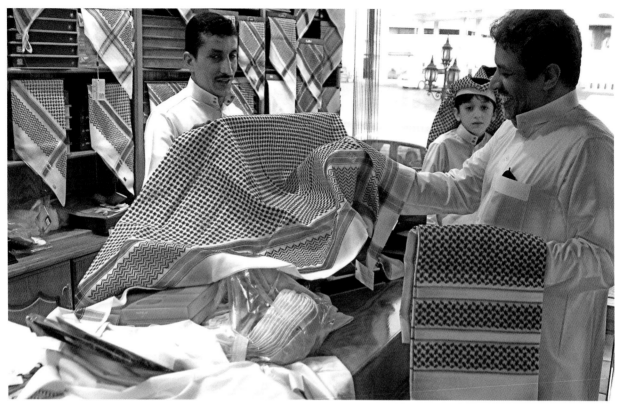

(including foreign nationals). The population in Saudi Arabia is also relatively young, with a median age of twenty-six years. And with the population's growth rate around 1.5 percent each year, the number of children will continue to increase.

A Saudi man and his son shop for a new headscarf in preparation for the Eid al-Fitr holiday.

NATIONAL DRESS: THOBE AND VEIL

The blistering sun of the desert and the conservative traditions of the nomads have combined to produce a striking combination of national dress—one style for men, another for women.

Saudi men generally wear a long white robe, called a *thobe* (THOH-bay), made of cotton for hot weather and light wool for cooler days. On the head is a skull cap, over which they drape a flowing head covering, or *gutra* (GOOT-rah). In summer, a light white gutra of cotton is preferred because it is cooler. In winter, a warmer, red-and-white checked version is worn. A heavy, doubled

Recently, abayas with small amounts of colorful embroidery against the black, like this one in Jeddah, have become acceptable for women's wear.

cord around the head, called *egal* (EE-gahl), often black and traditionally used to tie camels, secures the gutra in place.

Traditionally, a Bedouin man never felt well-dressed unless he was also well-armed. He usually carried a dagger, knife, sword, and spear. Later, rifles—together with leather bandoliers worn across the chest to hold cartridges for the rifles—replaced the spears. Today weapons are worn only for special ceremonial occasions.

The most distinctive feature of traditional Saudi dress for women is the veil. Practiced in the Middle East since at least 1500 BCE, face veiling has a practical purpose for women living in harsh desert environments—it protects a woman's face from the desert sun and windblown sand, although this practice differs regionally.

With the introduction of Islam, face veiling became more of a social norm than a practical one. It is a strict requirement for conservative Muslims who believe a woman must take every possible precaution to safeguard her modesty. This means not allowing men—except for relatives—to see her face, hair, or body. The veil is traditionally worn so that only the woman's eyes are visible.

In the last decade, many Saudi women in Jeddah, probably the most open and least conservative city in Saudi Arabia, have been going out of their homes unveiled. Even these comparatively liberated women, however, still take pains to make sure that they keep their head, hair, and body well-covered. They wear another striking and traditional piece—the *abaya* (ah-BAH-yah), a long, black outer cloak that drapes from head to ankle (except for part of the face, which is usually covered by a veil)—when they leave the privacy of home. Similar to the veil, the abaya serves to protect a woman's modesty.

Folklore from the Saudi past tells the story of a Bedouin sheikh who was known as the "Benefactor (Caretaker) of the Wolves." Whenever he heard a wolf howling near his tent, he would order a servant to take a goat out into the desert, tie it there, and then return to the camp. The reason: the sheikh insisted on being a good host. "No guest," he said, "shall call on me in the evening without dining." It would not be honorable, he felt, to let any guest—be it a camel or even a hungry wolf—leave his camp without being properly fed and given water to drink.

By greatly exaggerating the Saudi commitment to hospitality, this story points out the great importance of honor in Saudi culture. A desert warrior once remarked, "Bedouin can be roused to do anything for honor." Part of that custom includes the need to save face—in other words, the necessity of preserving one's honor at all costs. Therefore, even at the risk of bankrupting himself by his open-handed hospitality to all visitors, the sheikh felt he had to maintain his reputation as a generous host. Had he failed to do so, he would have been ashamed.

In the last few years some modern Saudi fashion designers have copied the long flowing lines of traditional women's clothing in the Kingdom and have created colorful, graceful modern dresses that are a blend of old and new.

SOCIAL CLASS

The Prophet Muhammad proclaimed that all people are "equal children of Adam" (referring to Adam, the Biblical first man created by God). Muhammad asserted that God does not pay attention to social rank or race but only to the sincerity of a person's beliefs and the works of charity performed during his or her lifetime. This belief in the fundamental equality of all is a cornerstone of Muslim social thought. Compared with many other societies in the world, there are surprisingly few overt signs of class distinction in Saudi Arabia today.

A Saudi man inspects the crop in an irrigated field. Foreign workers would have done the planting.

Nevertheless, social classes do exist. At the very top of the social pyramid is, as might be expected, the House of Saud itself, consisting of the many descendants of King Abdul Aziz. Next in line in the social hierarchy are the old merchant families. These families are often from Jeddah, and have amassed vast fortunes, which were derived from trade that predated the oil boom. Although they have money, they have little political power.

Below them is a growing middle class of educated people, small businessmen, and mid-ranking civil service officials. This group is becoming more important as national policies of "Saudization" (replacing foreign technicians with Saudi technicians) and diversification (developing sources of national income other than petroleum) begin to take hold. These officials are the Saudis with the most hands-on experience in the actual running of a modern state.

Manual labor is considered "dishonorable," and as a result, Saudis usually refuse to do it. There is no Saudi blue-collar working class in the cities. Manual labor is provided by migrant workers, who are sometimes treated like property. In rural areas, there are still the small farmers and in the deserts, the remaining nomads. These two interest groups may be at the lower rungs of the social ladder, but politically the royal family still needs their support to stay in power.

ADJUSTING TO RAPID TRANSFORMATION

Since the oil boom of the 1970s, Saudi Arabia has undergone rapid social change. From a simple background that saw little change over many centuries, the country had found great riches that propelled it forward into modern times, practically overnight.

In a period of little more than thirty years, Saudi Arabia built a nation that cares for its sick, educates its young, and provides a wide choice of industries in which its workforce can participate. Running water and electricity now reach even the most remote corners of the Kingdom.

It is a fascinating sociological study to see how the average Saudi has embraced the modern age while maintaining his or her traditions. While the nation's great wealth has brought rapid and widespread changes, the Saudi family has remained intact. Young Saudis cruise the Internet and play video games. The elderly are cared for within the family unit, and most Saudi mothers stay home to raise their children and take care of the family's needs, rather than working outside the home.

Women watch Saudi Arabia's Sarah Attar compete in the 2012 Olympics.

Another anchor of stability in this storm of change has been Saudi Arabia's government. The House of Saud led the country even before the Kingdom of Saudi Arabia was established in 1932, thereby providing continuity in government.

INTERNET LINKS

lightbox.time.com/2013/05/23/rich-nation-poor-people-saudi-arabia-by-lynsey-addario/#1
Time LightBox: *Rich Nation, Poor People*
This 2013 *Time* magazine photo gallery presents a rarely-seen side of Saudi Arabian society: the poor.

saudiarabia.angloinfo.com/AgloInfo
A site for foreign workers, or expats, working in Saudi Arabia, geared toward the Western, high-status worker. It offers insights on everyday life in the Kingdom.

LIFESTYLE

Two Saudi men walk past a distinctive building in Hail. The city is known for its historic mud-brick forts and towers.

7

SAUDI ARABIA'S RAPID twentieth-century transformation from remote desert kingdom to international power might have caused culture shock in its people. But the country's traditional values remained in place as the bedrock of Saudi society, providing constancy in the midst of change. Islam is not only a religion; it is a way of life. It defines the Saudi national character and culture, and guides every moment of a person's life.

FAMILY IS EVERYTHING

Since Biblical times, the family has been the only safe haven in the hostile environment of the Arabian Peninsula. It was not until the creation of the Kingdom of Saudi Arabia in 1932 that there was any central authority to keep the peace and punish transgressors. Under these conditions, the family became supremely important. Individuals simply could not survive without the support of others.

Traditionally, "family" meant the extended family. Covering at least three generations, the extended family usually included the father and mother, their unmarried children, and their married sons who had wives

Royal lifestyles vary a great deal. Some princes have huge palaces and lead extravagant jet-set lives. Others live modestly and devote themselves to business or good works. But all members of the royal family understand that their own well-being is directly related to the well-being of the House of Saud. They therefore cultivate and nurture family relationships, consulting other family members and getting their approval before making any major decisions.

and children of their own. Other relatives were often included, too. For example, a divorced woman could not live alone but would return to the house of her father or another male relative. A widow would move in with her son or son-in-law. These extended families were usually very close and very large.

In Saudi Arabia today, this pattern is changing. Married children may prefer to set up their own households if they can afford it. The classic three-generation extended family, all living under the same roof or in the same compound, is no longer the rule, especially in the cities. Nonetheless, the new, smaller nuclear family has managed to inherit at least four of the key characteristics of the traditional extended family.

A Saudi family admires a floral display during the Flower Festival in Riyadh.

TRADITIONAL FAMILY STRUCTURE

The traditional family structure that has been adopted by modern Saudi Arabians consists of the following traits, among others:

First is the central importance of the patriarch of the family. Descent is patrilineal—children are identified only through their father as *ibn* or *bin* Khalid (son of Khalid) or *bint* Khalid (daughter of Khalid)—and the oldest male is the unquestioned head of the family, the patriarch. When family decisions are made, he is the one who finally decides what should be done after hearing the views of other members of the family. The mother has a great behind-the-scenes influence on her family, but she is not the formal decision-maker.

A second trait is that the survival and prosperity of the family itself is considered to be much more important than the wishes of any individual in it.

The most dramatic example of the Saudi family as a source for mutual aid and protection is the royal family itself. There are no official figures for the number of people in the family, but estimates run from 6,000 to 15,000 or more. It is the largest, wealthiest, and most influential (in the country's domestic affairs) royal family in the world. Of the thousands of descendants of King Abdul Aziz, and their families, a core constituency holds most of the power and government positions.

The House of Saud takes pains to make sure that its foundations are firm to ensure the continuity of the family line. Although King Abdullah will remain the official ruler of Saudi Arabia until his death, his advanced age means the throne will soon be passed on to another. That will be his half-brother Crown Prince Salman. Power has been shared with a new generation, too. Abdullah's son, Mutaib bin Abdullah, is the minister of the National Guard. Abdullah's grandson, Prince Khalid bin Bandar Al Saud, is the governor of Riyadh Province. The late King Faisal's son Prince Saud bin Faisal bin Abdulaziz Al Saud is the Foreign Minister of Saudi Arabia. These arrangements at the most senior levels ensure that political and military power remain with the royal family.

Crown Prince Salman bin Abdul Aziz al-Saud

Thanks to its preeminent political position, the House of Saud is in a position to ensure that its financial position is secure. Their wealth supports their power and their power protects their wealth. That staggering wealth, however, must be spread around. Because King Abdul Aziz had so many children, the royal family is huge. All these people have a claim, great or small, to a share of the House of Saud's riches.

Because of his seniority, the patriarch is thought to be the one most able to identify the best interests of the group. Other family members are expected to go along with his decisions no matter what their personal feelings may be. The individualism found in the United States and some other Western cultures has no place in the Saudi way of life, particularly if it is expressed by women.

A third holdover from the days of the extended family is that most social activities take place only within the family. Traditionally Saudi families did not often go to restaurants or to public events such as fairs and festivals. Non-official entertaining was done at home, which offered the advantage of privacy. Additionally, keeping up with all the achievements and setbacks of parents, brothers, sisters, children, and other relatives is almost a full-time job. It requires a constant exchange of visits and does not leave much time for other social activities outside the family circle.

The final benefit of the extended family is the most important— personal security. The family is still the real safety net of Saudi society. It is a matter of family pride and honor that members take good care of one another. A person may be old, sick, unemployed, divorced, widowed, or handicapped— whatever the problem, the family will provide emotional support and money.

In the past the tribal families of the Arabian Peninsula used to play much the same social role, though on a bigger scale, as the extended family does today. Tribal leaders gave their followers moral and financial support in life and avenged them when they were killed in battle by other tribes. Over the past forty years, however, city life and the rapid economic development of the country have made these tribal ties less relevant to many Saudis.

A GROWING MIDDLE CLASS

Not all Saudis are princes or nomads. Many Saudi men and women are now well-educated and form a prosperous middle class. Often educated in the United States, they know the culture of the West, but prefer to live and work in their own country. Their lifestyle is much closer to the Western model than to the traditional Arabian one. This new educated middle class may be the bridge between the petroleum-based Saudi Arabia of today and the more diversified, technically-proficient Saudi Arabia of the future.

The Saudi middle class live in houses with a limited number of rooms or in apartments. They usually own these houses or apartments, borrowing money to pay for them from Saudi banks, which give generous loans for just this purpose. The men hold government jobs or else go into private business. In most cases, women stay home, caring for the children. If they choose to work, they are encouraged to have vocations in science, languages, and the arts.

Even though this group of people may study or work in the West for considerable periods of time, they continue to respect the religious teachings and customs of their own country. They know that their travels abroad are for specific purposes only. Once their goals have been achieved, almost all of them will return to the Kingdom. This basic faithfulness to their own traditions and values makes it easier for them to readjust to the restrictions of Saudi culture when they return to their homeland.

Visitors amble through the mall inside the Royal Clock Tower building in Mecca.

MEASURING TIME

Saudis have inherited from their nomadic past a very relaxed attitude toward most commitments based on time, such as business appointments, sporting events, and social engagements. In Saudi eyes, time is too often the master of Western culture. They themselves are much more comfortable with time as their servant. It is said that the "correct" time for a 10 a.m. meeting is not when the clock itself says 10 a.m., but when the participants themselves are able to get to the place where the meeting will be held.

This relaxed view about time is neatly summed up in the very common

Arabic phrase, *In sha' Allah* ("God willing"), as in "I will meet you at the hotel at 10 a.m., In sha' Allah."

Time in Saudi Arabia is measured by the Islamic calendar. It takes as its starting point the Hijrah (July 16, 622 CE), when Muhammad moved from Mecca to Medina. From this beginning, time is subsequently reckoned according to the lunar calendar, which has 354 days. Years are designated A.H., which stands for *Anno Hegirae*, Latin for "the year of the Hijrah." By using comparative tables, A.H. dates can be translated into CE dates (CE stands for Common Era, which is alternatively called A.D., or *Anno Domini,* "the year of the Lord," according to the Gregorian, or international, calendar). For example, the year 1435 A.H. corresponds to 2014 CE.

The weekend is also different in Saudi Arabia from what it is in the Western world. Because Friday is a day of rest and prayer, the weekend falls on Thursday and Friday, not on Saturday and Sunday. This fact is frequently forgotten by businessmen and officials in other countries, who sometimes try, unsuccessfully, to telephone their Saudi counterparts during the Saudi weekend.

Saudi students take their final high school exams in the city of Jeddah.

EDUCATION: AT HOME AND ABROAD

Traditionally education in Saudi Arabia involved memorizing and reciting large blocks of the Qur'an. Saudi educational policy today is still firmly grounded in the study of Islamic beliefs. It also tries to convince students that, since their country is providing free education for them (including generous scholarships to study abroad), they have a responsibility to support their country's traditions and policies.

Young Saudi women attend an English language class at the University of Colorado in Denver in 2012.

Before the oil boom, Saudi Arabia had a high level of illiteracy. In the 1970s the Kingdom began to build an impressive array of new schools, ranging from kindergartens to universities, staffed by Saudis and foreigners alike. Except at the kindergarten level, boys and girls may not go to school together. Boys' schooling consists of kindergarten, primary, intermediate, high school, and university. After the first year of high school, boys may specialize in either scientific or literary studies. There are also vocational schools offering courses in technical, agricultural, and business subjects. Advanced studies take place at numerous colleges and universities, of which the new Diriyah campus of King Saud University is the largest and best known.

The Saudi government also pays for bright students to study abroad. Many Saudis who go to college overseas do so in the West, often to the United States, and to a lesser extent, the United Kingdom.

The first school for girls in Saudi Arabia was set up in 1956. Before then, if girls received any formal education at all, it was from private tutors in their own homes. Today, more than half of the students attending Saudi universities and colleges are women. Since they cannot attend classes with men, closed-circuit television is used so that they can listen to male lecturers. There are also some all-female campuses.

THE CYCLE OF SAUDI LIFE

In nomadic life, parents valued boys more than girls. A boy grew into a warrior who could defend his own tribe. When he married, his wife and children became part of and strengthened his extended family. A girl, on the other hand, could not fight. After puberty, her sexual honor could be compromised, bringing shame to the family. When she married, she weakened the extended family by leaving it to join her husband's. The birth of a boy was therefore a cause for great celebration; the birth of a girl was met with much less enthusiasm.

The traditional preference for boys continues today. When a woman bears a son, she assumes a new title: *umm* (OOM), or "mother of," followed by her son's name. Until she has a son, she is only *bint* (BINT), or "daughter of," followed by her father's name. Boys get special treatment. They are breast-fed longer than girls and become the favorites of the *hareem* (hah-REEM) or "women's quarters." At the same time, girls are learning the subdued behavior considered appropriate for women.

As they grow up, however, boys come in for a rude shock. By the age of seven, they leave their childhood behind and become part of their father's world—a more disciplined world of men. Girls remain with the women, where they prepare for their future roles as wives and mothers.

MARRIAGE AND DIVORCE

In Saudi Arabia, men can have up to four wives at a time. The Qur'an says, however, that if a man feels he cannot treat all his wives with equal fairness, he should take only one. In Muhammad's time, polygamy (having more than one wife) helped the desert tribes survive. Warriors were often killed in battle, leaving women widowed and children fatherless. If men had not been allowed to marry these widows, both the widows and their children might have died.

Some societies, such as the United States, put a high value on personal freedom. Men and women are free to marry whomever they like. Saudi society, on the other hand, looks at marriage differently. The Saudis believe

WEDDINGS: WOMEN'S WORLD

A young woman almost always accepts as her husband the man her parents have chosen. Her wedding is the most important day in her life and is celebrated elaborately. Wedding expenses are sometimes exorbitant, but the cost is shared by both families.

The private, religious part of the wedding is performed separately and before the more public ceremonial events. In Islam, the marriage ceremony itself involves an imam, *or religious leader. He meets privately with the bride-to-be and asks her if she will accept the prospective husband. If she agrees, the imam later asks the groom, this time in the presence of four witnesses (who cannot be members of either family) if he will take the woman for his wife. If he says yes, this pronunciation, attested to by the witnesses, makes the marriage valid. The marriage contract is officially recorded by the imam.*

At wedding celebrations, held in the evening at the bride's home or in a hotel, male and female guests do not mix. The men never see the bride, since it is quite unacceptable socially for an unveiled Saudi woman to be seen by men who are not her close relatives. Many Saudi brides now wear Western-style white wedding gowns. During the party, the bride and groom make a formal appearance among the female guests to receive their congratulations.

WOMEN TAKE TO THE STREETS...IN CARS

On October 26, 2013, about twenty-five Saudi women in various cities around the Kingdom got behind the steering wheel of a car and went for a spin. They were protesting their country's ban on women drivers. Indeed, Saudi Arabia is the last country on Earth that does not allow women to drive. It wasn't the first such protest, nor was it the last.

As mass protests go, twenty-five is not a large number of participants. But some of the women posted videos of themselves driving on YouTube, so the world could see—and it did. Some of the female drivers were arrested and taken to police stations, where they had to wait for male relatives to come take them home. Others went unnoticed by authorities. Despite having to sign documents promising not to drive again, some of the activists said they intended to do exactly that again and again until the law is changed.

On a website for October 26 Women's Driving Campaign, tens of thousands signed an online petition calling for an end to the driving ban for women in Saudi Arabia.

the most important question about marriage is not about the personal happiness of the couple, but whether the marriage will strengthen the two families involved. Since this decision is too important to be left to a young man and young woman, almost all marriages are arranged by their parents.

A Saudi girl drives an ATV with her younger sister at a park near Riyadh in 2013. Saudi Arabia recently lifted the ban on women riding bicycles and motorbikes, but only in recreational areas while dressed in full Islamic veil and accompanied by a male relative.

Saudis tend to marry young, usually in their early twenties. (However, the tradition of older men marrying child brides, sometimes as young as six, continues in some places, and is cause for international condemnation.) The groom has to pay a "bride price" by giving jewelry or other goods to his bride worth an agreed-upon amount of money. These items are the bride's personal property. If the couple divorces, she gets to keep them. For a man, divorce is very easy. All he has to do is say "I divorce you" three times. He must then give to the wife whatever is hers under the marriage contract.

A woman may also divorce her husband, but this is more difficult and requires a divorce order by a religious leader.

A Saudi woman and her children get into a taxi in Riyadh. Women are banned from driving cars.

THE RESTRICTED WORLD OF SAUDI WOMEN

In a dramatic and unexpected move in 1990, a group of seventy veiled Saudi women defied the Kingdom's longstanding policy that women are not allowed to drive cars: they drove in a convoy of cars in Riyadh until the police stopped and detained them.

This remarkable demonstration for the right to drive was the first known public protest by Saudi women against the traditional role of women in the country. It would not be the last.

Why does Saudi Arabia set what Westerners feel are such severe limitations on the freedom of women? The answer lies in one of the most important social values in Saudi Arabia—honor. The honor of a man himself is inextricably bound up with the honor of the women of his family. In comparison with men, women are thought to be weaker and more subject to temptation.

The rules of behavior are so extremely rigid that a woman can jeopardize her sexual honor merely by talking to or sitting beside a man not related to her. Once violated, her honor can never be restored. Since the Qur'an teaches that men have authority over women, it is up to men to protect women. This is why women and men do not interact in public—to prevent any suggestion of inappropriate behavior that might shame a woman's family.

The result is that Saudi women are shielded by veil and social convention from all contact with men who are not their close relatives. They are not allowed to go to school with men, to work with men, to drive cars, or to appear in public dressed in a "provocative" manner, meaning without being fully shrouded in a black abaya. The socially preferred role for Saudi women is to be in the home. They are strongly encouraged to be wives, mothers, and homemakers. If women want to or must work, the most appropriate jobs for them are considered to be medical, social, or educational work, but only with women or girls as their patients, clients, or students.

These restrictions might not be tolerated by women in other societies, but so far, few Saudi women have protested these restrictions. For one thing, Saudi women have been brought up to accept this way of life as entirely normal, and they earn the approval of their husbands and their families if they do their duties well. For another, they simply have no alternative, except to leave the Kingdom and live and work in some other country. Also, by conforming to the demands of Saudi society, they are rewarded with a very high degree of personal, social, and financial security. And finally, consequences for non-conformity can be severe.

As more and more Saudi women study abroad and experience a freer lifestyle, however, the number of females willing to accept these restrictions may change.

INTERNET LINKS

english.alarabiya.net/News.html
Al Ararabiya News offers news, arts, and lifestyle stories from all Arab countries.

www.aawsat.net/
Asharq Al-Awsat is a pan-Arab daily newspaper. The website offers news, lifestyle and culture features, sports, and more.

hopeinterculturalcomm.weebly.com
Connections—an in-depth guide offering insights into Saudi culture from young peoples' perspective.

ideas.time.com/2013/10/25/forbidden-to-drive-a-saudi-woman-on-life-inside-the-kingdom
Forbidden to Drive: A Saudi Woman On Life Inside the Kingdom
A first-hand account, with video, by a Saudi woman.

nidalm.com/blog/photoshoots/weddings-in-saudi-arabia
A well-done blog photo essay by a professional photographer shows the men's side of a Saudi wedding celebration.

www.nytimes.com/2008/05/13/world/middleeast/13girls.html
Love on Girls' Side of the Saudi Divide
www.nytimes.com/2008/05/12/world/middleeast/12saudi.html
Young Saudis, Vexed and Entranced by Love's Rules
A look at the divided worlds of young Saudi men and women.

RELIGION

A child practices reciting holy verses.

8

SLAM IS THE SECOND-LARGEST religion in the world, after Christianity. Some 1.6 billion people, or 23.4 percent of the world population, are Muslims. *Islam* in Arabic means "submission (to God)." *Muslims* are the believers, or followers, of Islam. Saudi Arabia is the birthplace of Islam and continues to function as its heart and soul today, and almost all Saudis are practicing Muslims. The country is home to Mecca and Medina, Islam's two most sacred cities—and the destinations of millions of devout pilgrims each year. Faithful Muslims the world over direct their daily prayers toward Mecca.

It would be very hard to exaggerate the importance of religion in Saudi Arabia today. The opening words of all official government documents are the opening words of the Qur'an: "In the name of Allah, the Compassionate, the Merciful." The flag of the Kingdom bears the Muslim's declaration of faith: "There is no god but God; Muhammad is the Messenger of God."

One of the most common Saudi expressions is "*Alhamdulillah*" (ahl-HAHM-doo-lee-lah), meaning "Thanks be to God." No religion but Islam

" And hold fast, all of you together, to the faith of Allah, and do not separate. And remember Allah's favor unto you: how you were enemies and he made friendship between your hearts so that you became as brothers by his grace ..."
–a quote from the Qur'an, III: #103

A variety of Islamic literature is for sale in the main *souk*, or traditional market, in Jeddah.

may be openly practiced in Saudi Arabia. And virtually everybody in Saudi Arabia, except for desert travelers, hears the melodious call to prayer five times daily.

A TOTAL WAY OF LIFE

Islam is more than just a religion; it's a total way of life. Saudi culture in particular adheres to a very strict interpretation of Islam called *Wahhabism*. Islam permeates through all levels and aspects of society to the individuals themselves. Islam encourages a sense of brotherhood through a shared faith. It provides a set of regulations governing all aspects of family life and offers clear guidelines on personal behavior and legal matters. As a result, devout Muslims feel that they can find in Islam the answers to many of the pressing questions of everyday life.

Moreover, in Saudi Arabia there is no clear distinction, as there is in the United States and other countries, between church and state. The two are deeply intertwined; Saudi Arabia is an Islamic state governed by Islamic law and administered through Islamic social institutions.

BASIC BELIEFS: GOD AND HUMANITY

Saudi Arabia is the cradle of Islam. Compared with the polytheistic (featuring multiple gods) beliefs it replaced, the religion introduced by the Prophet Muhammad brought many social reforms and different ethical standards to Arabian society.

ONE GOD Muslims believe that there is only one God, who created and sustains the world. Muhammad himself was not divine but the last and greatest of a series of prophets. Jesus Christ, Abraham, and Moses are also revered as prophets in Islam.

PARADISE One of the prophet Muhammad's main teachings was that no matter how old one is or what one's past sins have been, it is never too late to repent and ask God for forgiveness. Islam teaches that God judges everyone by their behavior during their lives. Those who live meritorious lives will get to enjoy the pleasures of heaven, which, with bountiful food and endless streams of pure water, is just the opposite of the harsh daily life of the desert.

CHARITY Bound together by their common faith, Muslims should ideally be, according to Islam, a caring community. Islam stresses the importance of works of charity to ease human suffering, such as giving money to the poor. Muhammad himself had directed his followers to pay special attention to those who were in the greatest need in his own time: women, orphans, and slaves. Lending money and charging interest (a practice called *usury*), which is the normal system in the West, is forbidden in Saudi Arabia.

The "Floating Mosque" in Jeddah is built over the water in the Red Sea. At high tide, the mosque appears to be floating.

WRITINGS OF ISLAM

Knowing something about the famous scriptures of Islam—the Qur'an and the Hadith—also helps with understanding this religion.

THE QUR'AN The Qur'an is to Muslims a divinely-inspired, never-failing source of religious instruction and literary excellence. It is considered by Muslims to be the direct word of God, brought to Muhammad in small increments by the angel Gabriel over a period of twenty years. Muhammad received these messages from God through visions, and he would recite aloud to his followers what had been revealed to him.

Initially recorded by his disciples on whatever materials were conveniently at hand—pieces of paper, stones, palm leaves, bits of leather, camel bones— these recitations were assembled into the Qur'an, which consists of 114 chapters, called *surah* (SOO-rah), of different lengths. The chapters have short titles, such as "The Cow," which refer to creatures or people mentioned in the surah itself. Some of the surah are brief, poetic statements. Others

The prayer ritual includes touching the forehead to the ground in the direction of Mecca.

are longer and more complex. After the death of Muhammad in 632 CE, Muslims felt the need for an agreed-upon text of the Qur'an. Islamic scholars compiled pieces from different sources, and produced an authoritative text of the sacred book.

THE HADITH With the text of the Qur'an decided once and for all, scholars could turn their attention to the sayings and traditions surrounding the Prophet Muhammad himself. These are collectively known as the *Hadith* (hah-DEETH), which means a report or a record of sayings or actions. They offer detailed guidance to the faithful on almost all day-to-day activities of life, from how one washes oneself to how to forgive other people for wrongdoing by referring to the example of the Prophet and how he lived his life.

In the Hadith, tricky moral questions are asked and then cleverly answered. Here is a good example: A man bought a piece of land and unexpectedly found a pot of gold buried there. Rather than secretly keeping the gold for himself, he immediately told the former owner about it. But the former owner refused the buyer's claim to the gold, saying that it had not been part of their bargain. The solution, which was proposed by a third man called in to solve the problem, was truly creative: The son of the new owner should marry the daughter of the former owner. In that way, the young couple could then be given the gold as their wedding present.

THE FIVE PILLARS OF ISLAM

After Muhammad died, his followers began to define more formally what it meant to be a Muslim. They identified five key duties for members of the faith. Known as the Pillars of Islam, these are duties that every Muslim has to fulfill if he or she is able to.

The five pillars are: a declaration of faith, daily prayers, helping the poor, fasting, and a pilgrimage.

DECLARATION OF FAITH To become a Muslim, one must recite aloud a formal profession of faith, the *shahadah* (shah-HAH-dah): "There is no god but God; Muhammad is the Messenger of God." This is the first pillar. Once

Religious laws and customs in Saudi Arabia are rigidly enforced at the street level and in the souq *(SOOK), or marketplace, by the* mutawa *(MOO-tah-wah), or religious police.*

Working for the politically influential Committee for the Propogation of Virtue and the Prevention of Vice, the mutawa are often older men with henna-dyed beards, who carry a camel whip as a token of office. Semi-educated younger men who reject Western culture are also in its ranks.

The mutawa are strict Muslims whose job is to make sure that stores close promptly at prayer times and that women appearing in public are properly dressed. A woman who is not wearing an ankle-length skirt or whose arms or legs are visible may get a whipping on her legs or arms from one of the mutawa to warn her against such "immodest" behavior in the future.

done, this act makes a person a member of the believing community, and allows one to share fully in its religious creed and its daily way of life.

DAILY PRAYERS Praying five times a day is the second pillar. Believers are urged to pray together with others, but praying alone is also permitted if there is no alternative. The precise time for prayers changes daily, but they are always offered five times a day: before sunrise, in the early afternoon, in the late afternoon, after sunset, and before going to sleep.

Muslims can pray virtually anywhere: in the mosques, at home, in the desert, or at their places of work. In the afternoon, for example, it is common to see a row of praying men facing Mecca just outside the supermarkets of Saudi Arabia carrying out in unison the prescribed bows and prostrations of their prayers. Men can also pray in the aisle of an airplane, even when the plane is in flight. Women usually pray at home.

Attendance is encouraged at a weekly prayer service held at the mosques early on Friday afternoon. Here the imam, the leader of the service, takes a text from the Qur'an and elaborates on it in what can be a long, emotional sermon.

HELPING THE POOR The third pillar involves serving God by serving the needy. Known as *zakat* (ZAH-kaht), this act of social responsibility is fulfilled by donating a part of one's income to the poor. Normally it is 2.5 percent of an individual's net income annually. All Muslims are supposed to pay this tax, but since there are no penalties for failing to do so, it has become a voluntary offering.

FASTING The ninth month of the Muslim lunar calendar—which varies from year to year—is known as Ramadan. Fasting during the daylight hours of Ramadan constitutes the fourth pillar. (Since there were no clocks in the desert, early Muslims judged the exact time of sunrise as the moment when a white thread could be distinguished from a black one.) No eating, drinking, smoking, or sexual activities are permitted during the hours of the fast. Children, pregnant women, those who are ill, and those who are traveling are not obligated to fast.

A man and his son walk toward Mecca for the Hajj.

THE PILGRIMAGE The fifth and last pillar of Islam is the *hajj*, the pilgrimage to Mecca all Muslims should make at least once if their health permits it, and if they can afford it. Each year, more than 2 million Muslims from all over the world converge on Mecca by air, sea, and land to participate in one of the world's greatest pilgrimages. When Muslims have completed this pilgrimage, they are entitled to be known by the honorable title of *hajji* for men or *hajjah* for women.

RITES OF THE HAJJ

There are two kinds of pilgrimage to Mecca, Islam's most sacred city: the shorter *umrah* (OOM-rah) or visit, which can be done at any time of the year, and the hajj itself, which has a more elaborate ritual and takes place only

After dawn prayer, Muslim pilgrims walk around the Ka'bah inside the Grand Mosque of Mecca.

once a year. The rites of the hajj require about 12 days to complete, but many pilgrims stay on longer to visit the other holy city, Medina.

As a first step of the hajj, before entering Mecca, the pilgrims put on special clothes signifying their holy state and their equality before God. For a man this outfit consists of white toweling and sandals; the only requirement for a woman is that her attire be modest and she may not wear gloves nor certain types of veils. The pilgrims must also chant to God, showing acceptance of the rituals that lie ahead.

Entering the Grand Mosque of Mecca, the pilgrim walks seven times counter-clockwise around the Ka'bah, a square building. In it is set the Black Stone, a sacred relic believed by the faithful to date from the time of the biblical Abraham. Pilgrims kiss or gesture toward the stone, which is believed to be able to absorb their sins. Other rites include drinking from the holy waters of the Well of Zamzam and a ritualized running (more like a brisk walk) between two low hills.

The culmination of the hajj, however, is the Standing on the Plain of Arafat, where pilgrims stand all afternoon reading from the Qur'an and repeating the prayer, "Here I am, O God, here I am!" The next day they gather pebbles to throw at three stone pillars, crying, *"Allahu Akbar"* (ah-LAH-hoo akh-bar), "God is most great!" Casting the stones symbolizes the casting out of evil. On the tenth day of the hajj, men shave their heads, and women cut a few stands of their hair. To commemorate Abraham's sacrifice of his son Ishmael, sheep or goats are sacrificed and the meat is given to the poor.

At mosques around the world men and women are usually segregated, but during the hajj, both sexes may walk and pray together. Women, however, must be accompanied by a husband, a male relative, or by at least one other pious woman when they perform the hajj.

THE GREAT MOSQUES OF THE KINGDOM

From very modest beginnings, the great mosques of Saudi Arabia—the Quba Mosque near Medina, the Prophet's Mosque in Medina, and the Grand Mosque

The Grand Mosque welcomes spiritual pilgrims to Mecca.

of Mecca—have evolved into glorious destinations. They are at the same time places of prayer and centers for education.

Because Muslims are required to pray five times a day, mosques were traditionally built where most people congregated, in the middle of towns or near markets. Mosques vary in size and architectural design, but they have similar parts. The inner area of the mosque is designed for worship. The outer courtyard can also be used for prayers if the mosque itself is crowded.

Since Muslims are to pray facing the Ka'bah in Mecca, a *mihrab*, a recess in the mosque, shows the direction of Mecca. On Friday, sermons are given from a high pulpit inside the mosque. The melodious call to prayer is made from a tall minaret overlooking the mosque. In the past, the call was made by a *muezzin* (moo-EZ-in) with a far-reaching voice. Today the muezzin uses loudspeakers.

The Quba Mosque, Islam's first mosque, was built by Muhammad in 622 before he entered Medina from Mecca. It has been upgraded many times,

Giant canopies provide shade at the Masjid Nabawi, or Prophet's Mosque, compound in Medina.

most recently by King Fahd in the early 1990s. In Medina, Muhammad built a second mosque, the Prophet's Mosque, named after him. It, too, has been improved many times. In the late 1800s, for example, a prayer hall and ornate colonnades were added.

Impressive as these two mosques are, however, the Grand Mosque of Mecca is the spiritual heart of Islam. It contains the Ka'bah, a cubic stone structure about 45 feet (14 m) high and 30 feet (9 m) wide, which is located in the center of the mosque. A huge black silk cloth, the *Kiswah* (KIS-wah), which is embroidered in gold with verses from the Qur'an, is draped over the Ka'bah and is replaced every year. Flanked by minarets 270 feet (82 m) high and often renewed and expanded, the Grand Mosque is a masterpiece of Islamic taste, craftsmanship, and design.

INTERNET LINKS

www.bbc.co.uk/religion/religions/islam/
BBC Religions: Islam
An easy to navigate site that provides a broad introduction to the religion and culture.

www.pbs.org/empires/islam/index.html
Muhammad: Legacy of a Prophet

www.pbs.org/empires/islam/index.html
Islam: Empire of Faith
These companion websites offer supporting content to accompany the videos, which are available as DVDs. However, much of the content is excellent on its own.

www.nytimes.com/2009/01/03/world/middleeast/03preacher.html
"Preaching Moderate Islam and Becoming a TV Star"
A surprising look at a new generation of television preachers in Saudi Arabia.

LANGUAGE

Saudi TV, with its headquarters in Riyadh, is the official government-owned television station.

9

HAL TATAKALLAM AL-LUGHA AL-ARABIYA? "Do you speak Arabic?" Some 280 million people, or more than 4 percent of the world's population, speak it as their native language. Arabic is the fifth-most commonly spoken language in the world. Just like the Arabian people themselves, the language evolved on the Arabian Peninsula. It is a Semitic language, like Hebrew, and the roots of these languages go back thousands of years. Today Arabic has many variations that are used across North Africa and the Middle East.

Many Saudis believe that Arabic has a special importance because it is the language of the Qur'an. The verbal richness of the Qur'an has, for the Saudis, set a world standard for literary elegance. The wide range of subtle meanings that Arabic can express makes this language especially well-suited to poetry.

Arabic has two basic forms. The first is classical (written, or literary) Arabic, which is the same throughout the whole Arab world. The second, spoken Arabic, varies considerably from one region to another. Translating Arabic words into other languages is quite difficult because the sound system of Arabic is very different from English and other European languages. Moreover, some of the sounds commonly used

Here are some
Arabic words for
family members:
Father: *Ab*
Dad: *Baba*
Mother: *Umm*
Mom: *Mama*
Brother: *Akh*
Sister: *Akht*
Son (of): *Ibn*
Daughter (of):
Bint
Grandfather:
Jadd
Grandmother:
Jaddah

in Arabic are never used in Western languages. As a result, there are several possible ways in English to spell the same Arabic word, although some are seen as more authentic by Arabs. For example, "Moslem" and "Muslim" are both used, but "Muslim" is the preferred usage. "Muhammad" is also seen as "Mohammed."

Rock carvings by prehistoric nomads, such as these in the Nafud Desert, are still being discovered and documented in Saudi Arabia.

"Saud" might be more accurately represented in English as "Sa'ood," with two syllables. One author found no fewer than sixteen different spellings for the Red Sea port of Jeddah.

THE ARABIC ALPHABET, CALLIGRAPHY, AND NUMBERS

The Arabic alphabet was probably invented in the fourth century CE. Thanks to the rapid advance of the Arab Empire after the death of Muhammad, the Arabic alphabet spread quickly and is now the second-most widely used alphabet in the world—the Latin alphabet is the most common.

The Arabic alphabet has twenty-eight letters and is written and read from right to the left. The earliest copies of the Qur'an were written in a heavy, monumental script known as Kufi. Around 1000 CE, however, this style was replaced by Naskhi, a lighter script widely used in Saudi Arabia today. The form of this script is cursive, or a flowing style of writing that joins letters together.

In Saudi Arabia and other Islamic countries, calligraphy is a highly valued art because it is often used to copy the Qur'an. Calligraphers writing in Arabic

The calligraphic
Arabic script reads
from right to left.

use a reed pen with an angled point. This point lets them make bold down strokes, narrow upstrokes, and all the variations between.

Kufi, Naskhi, and other regional scripts lend themselves well to calligraphy, whether written on paper or employed to adorn the walls of mosques and other buildings. In these latter cases, verses from the Qur'an are often carved into the walls or written on tiles, which are then glazed and set in the walls.

Many English words come from Arabic such as *alchemy, alcohol, algebra, alkali, arsenal, assassin, azimuth, cipher, coffee, elixir, nadir, mosque, sugar, syrup,* and *zero.* The numbers *0, 1, 2, 3, 4, 5, 6, 7, 8, 9,* are known as Arabic numerals. The Arabs initially learned them from the Indians and later passed them on to the West.

PERSONAL NAMES

Saudis may give a child as many as four names: his or her own name, the father's and grandfather's names, and a tribal or family name.

Little boys like these might be named Ahmed, Omar, or Kamal.

There is a wide range of personal names. Some typical names for Bedouin men are Khalaf, Sattam, Nayif, Mit'ib, and Rakan; some typical names for Bedouin women are Sitih, Wadha, Joza, Amsha, and Salma.

Among the settled, non-Bedouin Saudis, men's names include Salim, Salman, Nasir, Salih, and Saif; women's names include Miznih, Hissih, Haya, Mudi, and Zainab.

There are no family names as such among the nomads. Each person takes the name of the clan or tribe as his or her last name. Examples of such names are Al Harbi, Al Shammari, and Al Marri. Among the settled Saudis, however, family names are the rule, for example, Al Gublan, Al Jabir, and Al Bassam. ("Al" in this context means "dynasty" or "house of." Thus "Al Saud" means "House of Saud," the name of the royal family.)

A Saudi man might be known as Muhammad bin Ahmad Al Sudairi (Muhammad, son of Ahmad of the Sudairi family), but in practice, he may be addressed simply as Muhammad or Mr. Al Sudairi. A woman takes her father's name and keeps it all her life, even after marriage. If she bears a son, umm is added to her name, followed by the name of her son, for example, umm Ali (mother of Ali).

BODY LANGUAGE

Within the circle of their extended family and with friends of their own sex, Saudis are warm, open people. Saudi men greet each other enthusiastically and may hold hands while walking together along a street—this is an expression of friendship. But in the presence of strangers, Saudis are usually much more restrained and are not given to any public displays of emotion.

When he shakes hands, a Saudi man prefers a short, limp handshake rather than a long, bone-crushing grip. After shaking hands with another Saudi, he may briefly bring his right hand to touch his heart as a show of his sincerity.

It's customary for Saudi boys and men to walk hand in hand.

When a Saudi man meets another Arabic speaker, he will probably greet him with the traditional welcome, "*as-salam alaykum*" (as-sahl-lahm ah-LAY-koom), or "peace be upon you." The traditional response is "*wa-alaykum as-salam,*" meaning "and to you be peace."

Outside the extended family, men and women interact in separate social circles. When a husband and wife go to a party, the husband joins the men in one part of the house, while the woman joins the other women elsewhere. Outside their homes, Saudi men and women never mingle with the opposite sex. Public displays of affection, even between husband and wife, are strictly forbidden.

THE MEDIA

Saudi law states that the role of the media is to educate and inspire national unity. The press, radio, and television are not free as in the United States, but are subject to government censorship. The government does not tolerate any criticism of Islam. "Pornography" such as advertisements showing women models wearing underwear, is prohibited. References to Christianity and other religions, pork, alcohol, and sex are routinely removed.

A woman journalist works at the headquarters of the Arab News in Jeddah. Women there can intermix with male professionals, but must wear an abaya and veil.

There are several daily and weekly Arabic newspapers. Most are privately owned but are subsidized and regulated by the government. Aware of the basic role played by the information media in encouraging participation in development projects and in educating the citizens about their responsibilities and national duty, the government has made ample provisions for radio and television services. In other words, television and radio stations are completely state owned and controlled. Programs now reach 90 percent of the country's population. Many of the programs are religious and literary in nature.

Most Saudis have satellite dishes that bring them uncensored news and entertainment programs from all parts of the world. The American news channel CNN is also widely viewed throughout the Kingdom. And more than 9.8 million Saudis have access to information on the Internet, while the country has one of the highest percentages of smartphone users in the world.

LANGUAGES OTHER THAN ARABIC

Because of Saudi Arabia's relationship with Britain and the United States, English is widely spoken by educated Saudis, including military officers and merchants. Many of the foreign workers in the Kingdom do not speak Arabic, but do speak at least some English. As a result, since the 1970s English has become the *lingua franca* (common tongue) of business, aviation, medicine, transportation, and communications.

INTERNET LINKS

www.al-bab.com
Al-Bab: An Open Door to the Arab World
Click on Arab language for an overview.

www.saudinf.com/main/g5.htm
SAMIRAD (Saudi Arabian Market Information Resource and Directory)
Click on "communications" for basic information about phone, postal and internet use.

en.rsf.org/report-saudi-arabia,146.html
Reporters without Borders
This group evaluates countries in terms of freedom of speech and media.

ARTS

Fiber arts, such as weaving and embroidery, have long been part of the women's domain in Arabian life.

10

THE MOST MAGNIFICENT ART IN Saudi Arabia must surely be the architecture of its mosques. The Grand Mosque in Mecca and the Floating Mosque of Jeddah are spectacular sights to behold. From the traditional, gleaming white Quba Mosque in Medina to the modern Great Mosque of Riyadh, built in 1992, the beauty of these buildings is equal to the role they play in Muslim life.

Outdoor art adorns a seaside street in Jeddah.

In 2013, Saudi Arabia entered a film as its first ever submission to the Academy Awards, in the foreign language category. The movie, *Wadjda*, was secretly written and directed by a Saudi woman, Haifaa Mansour. Saudi Arabia has no film industry. The story is about a ten-year-old girl who is determined to buy herself a bicycle that she is forbidden by law to ride.

Mosques and poetry are Saudi Arabia's two important contributions to the arts of the world. One thing that won't be found in the Kingdom, however, is a portrait gallery. The fine arts are restricted by a principle known as *aniconism*—the religious prohibition of representing any living creature by painting, sculpture, or other means. This prohibition stems from an Islamic belief that only God can create life.

There are no fine arts colleges or contemporary art museums in Saudi Arabia. A small group of young artists is trying to change that.

According to the conservative Saudi interpretation of this belief, an artist who produces an image of a living creature is trying to act like God. Saudi conservatives also fear that images might become idols and people might focus attention on the images rather than on God.

Some Muslim countries have not always rigorously followed the guiding principle of aniconism, but Saudi Arabia has always taken an uncompromising stand. Saudi purists also frown on large-scale public presentations of drama, fiction, songs, or instrumental music. As a result, the intellectual side of Saudi life is dominated by the spoken and written word and by Islam.

The nomadic life of the Saudis imposed its own strict logistical limitations on art since a Bedouin could own only what he could carry on his camel. Transporting paintings, drawings, or carvings from one grazing ground to another on camels would have been impractical.

STORYTELLERS AND POETS OF THE DESERT

In pre-Islamic days, poetry was the highest form of art in the Arabian Peninsula, appreciated and loved by the nomads.

A rich oral tradition was part of the Bedouin culture. Tales of personal exploits and tribal conquests were passed down from generation to generation through stories, often in the form of poetry. These tales played an important role in preserving and shaping Bedouin history. Over time storytelling and poetry became a Bedouin heritage and legacy. Words were a nomad's favorite form of artistic expression. To be a poet was to hold a post of great honor. According to an eleventh-century Muslim writer, whenever a poet emerged in an Arab tribe, other tribes would come and offer congratulations, for the poet was a defense to their honor, a protection of their good repute. He immortalized deeds of glory and published their eternal fame.

In the poverty of desert life, a man who could string words together in mystical chains telling tales of bygone days in a way that sang to the heart rather than the mind was indeed a man deserving of praise.

THE FUNCTIONAL ROLE OF THE ARTS

Given the prohibition on representational art, traditional Saudi artisans turned their attention instead to making everyday functional objects more beautiful. Objects in daily use were carefully made and were decorated with geometric, floral, and calligraphic designs.

Brass coffeepots exhibit typical Saudi craftsmanship.

For example, handsome wooden incense burners perfumed tents and houses with the smoke of frankincense; graceful brass water jugs were used to rinse the right hand before eating; roasted coffee beans and cardamom seeds were pounded in sturdy, elegant brass mortars; the resulting mixture was boiled in intricately decorated brass coffeepots; big wooden trays three feet in diameter were used to serve mutton and rice at banquets; chests, bowls, saddle frames, and other items made of wood were embellished with brass or silver nails; prayer beads made from materials gathered from around the world were traded in Mecca; house doors were ornately carved with geometric designs; narrow-necked pottery urns stored water or food; decorated leather goods, mats, and baskets, all well-suited to the tasks at hand, were also produced.

WEAVING AND EMBROIDERY

If poetry was a nomadic man's art, weaving and embroidery were part of the nomadic woman's world. Woven items were essential to nomadic life. Women made richly decorated riding litters, saddlebags, and tasseled blankets to use when traveling on camels. Woolen cloaks kept out the winter cold. Dresses were made from hand-loomed textiles. Carpets formed a floor for the tent, kept the sand at bay, and added touches of vivid color to the monochrome brown of desert life.

Embroidery was traditionally a skill learned by all young women. In the past almost all clothing in the Arabian Peninsula was embroidered by hand. Since the invention of the sewing machine, hand embroidery has given way to machine work.

The huge *Kiswah* (the ornate black cloth draped over the Ka'bah), which was formerly made in Egypt every year and presented to Saudi Arabia, is the largest, most important embroidered item now produced in the Kingdom. Each year, a new Kiswah is made by skilled embroiderers, using gold and silver metal thread on black velvet. The pattern consists of exquisite, flowing calligraphy of verses from the Qur'an, which is surrounded by interlaced patterns of leaves.

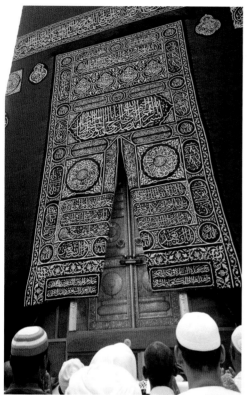

The immense, black velvet Kiswah is intricately embroidered in gold and silver. Each new cloth costs about $4.5 million.

BEDOUIN JEWELRY

In a nomadic society without banks and with few material possessions, a woman's wealth was in her jewelry. A Bedouin woman received most of her jewelry when she married. Usually made from silver and studded with turquoise and red stones, it was melted down upon her death, to be recast later as new pieces in other traditional designs.

Bedouin jewelry comes in the form of ornate necklaces, bracelets, armlets, anklets, belts, nose and ear ornaments, and finger-rings and toe-rings. These are still made in Saudi Arabia by silversmiths, using techniques that have not

THE ARDAH (THE SWORD DANCE)

The ardah (ahr-DAH) is a traditional Arabian dance that is performed in public places on religious and festive occasions.

The dancers, all men, are dressed in flowing white robes and armed with long swords. They stamp heavily and flash their swords, hopping from one foot to another in time to the beats and rhythms of the accompanying drums and tambourines.

As part of the performance, girls under twelve years old ululate, or utter high-pitched, wordless wailing. Wearing long bright dresses, they sway in time to the music and flick their long hair, which is heavily ornamented with beads, from side to side.

The audience may clap along or even join in the dance. When male members of the royal family are present they sometimes join the ardah dancers. When they do, they not only enjoy themselves, but they pay public tribute to the memory of how their ancestor, King Abdul Aziz, won Saudi Arabia—by the sword.

The dance has its origins in the Najd. Today the government of Saudi Arabia has set up several cultural institutions that promote and preserve Saudi Arabia's rich cultural heritage. The ardah dance is also performed in theaters.

changed much for hundreds of years. Metal is annealed, meaning it is heated and then gradually cooled to make it soft and malleable. Then it is fused, cast, hammered, embossed, or engraved. Silver jewelry is often ornamented with filigree work—thin wire twisted into delicate patterns and soldered into place.

New jewelry is sold by the weight of its silver and stones, not by its workmanship. Imported machine-made items, being much cheaper to

The Al-Hijr
Archaeological Site,
also called Madain
Saleh, was the
first place in Saudi
Arabia to become
a UNESCO World
Heritage property.

manufacture than handmade Bedouin jewelry, have in recent years been pricing traditional jewelry out of the market. Nevertheless, a good deal of used traditional jewelry is still available in the souq of Riyadh. Bargaining for it is a favorite pastime of many foreign residents.

ARCHITECTURE OF THE PAST

The most dramatic ancient ruins in Saudi Arabia are the well-preserved tombs and buildings carved into solid rock at Madain Saleh in the northwest of the country. These are more than 2,000 years old and were built by the Nabateans, an ancient nomadic people who once prospered as middlemen in the Arabian Peninsula's spice trade.

During the early years of Islam, architecture was simple and functional. Mosques began as minimal structures and only later evolved into their present glory. In the past only wealthy people had houses made of stone. Everyone else had to be content with homes made of sun-dried mud bricks, which were cheap to make, easy to repair, and kept dwellings cool in the summer and warm in the winter. Roof structures were usually made of tamarisk. Thick-walled forts and palaces were also made of coarse, sun-baked mud bricks, which were durable and strong. The historic fortified palace in Riyadh, Qasr al-Masmak (Masmak Fort), which Abdul Aziz captured in 1902, is a good example.

THE TALLEST BUILDING IN THE WORLD

The Kingdom Tower, currently under construction in Jeddah, was originally designed to be a mile high. It has since been scaled down a bit, to 3,280 feet (1,000 meters). That's two-thirds of a mile. If it is completed as planned, it will be the highest building in the world—taller than the current record-holder, the Burj Khalifa in Dubai, which stands at 2,717 feet (828 m.). It will dwarf the new One World Trade Center building in New York City—built on the site of the September 11, 2001, terror attacks—now the highest building in the United States at a symbolic 1,776 feet (541 m.)

Construction on the Kingdom Tower began in 2013. Supporters of the project hail it as a visionary economic investment, while critics say it's a symbol of arrogance. The building, which will contain office, retail, and living spaces, as well as the world's highest observation deck, is expected to take about five years to complete.

INTERNET LINKS

www.kingdomtowerskyscraper.com
Official site of the Kingdom Tower construction project.

www.saudiaramcoworld.com
Saudi Aramco World magazine is published in Houston, Texas, in collaboration with the oil company. It is an excellent source of English language stories about Saudi arts and culture.

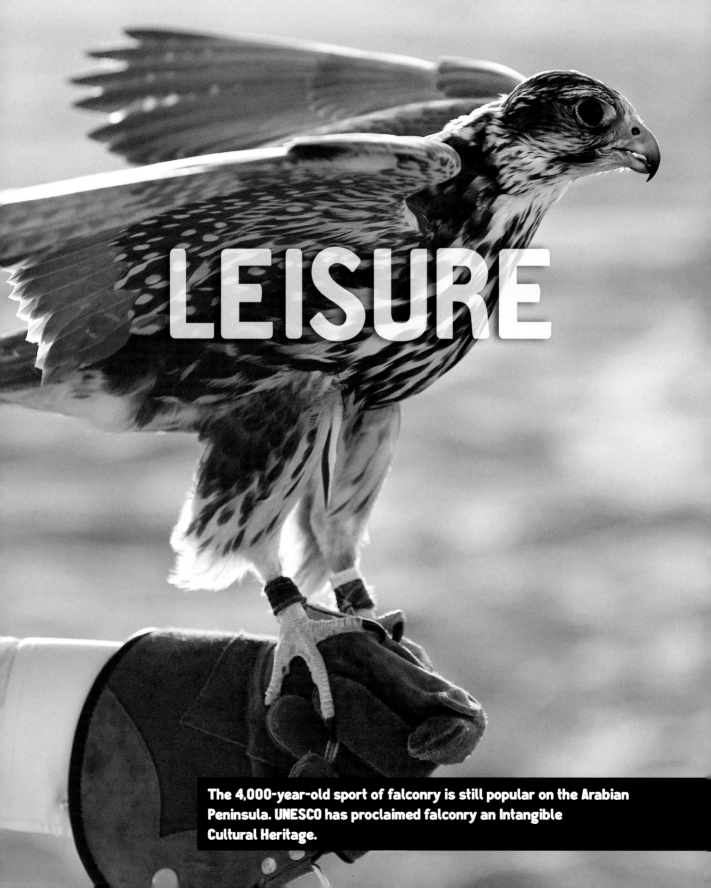

LEISURE

The 4,000-year-old sport of falconry is still popular on the Arabian Peninsula. UNESCO has proclaimed falconry an Intangible Cultural Heritage.

11

I N ANY SOCIETY, MOST PEOPLE HAVE to work. Whether the work is physically strenuous or mentally draining—or both—it's how people use their energy to meet their own needs and the needs of others. After all, no society can function without having somebody to grow the food, make the clothing, educate the children, heal the sick, and so forth. But perhaps nothing defines a people better than the ways in which they spend their nonworking hours.

For Saudis most entertainment takes place in the home and involves the family and relatives. There is not much public entertainment in Saudi Arabia. There are no pubs or bars because alcohol is banned under Islam. Saudi men and women are not supposed to mix socially, which rules out movies, restaurants, plays, art exhibitions, and many other cultural activities that adults of both sexes might conceivably attend.

Spending time with one's own family, keeping in close contact with other members of the extended family, celebrating birthdays, arranging marriages, catching up on the latest family gossip, and watching television and videos—these are favorite Saudi pastimes. Some Saudis participate in sports, and those who can afford it take vacation trips to countries with a cooler climate.

Camping is a popular leisure time activity for Saudis. Perhaps their heritage as desert nomads is in the blood. Many Saudi families pitch a tent in the desert, along the coast, or in a national park to enjoy the great outdoors.

A racing camel can
reach speeds of
20-25 miles (32-40
km) per hour.

TRADITIONAL SPORTS

The major sports of the Saudis, during the days when most of them were nomads, were all related to the desert. Favorite traditional sports today include camel racing, horseracing, and falconry.

The Bedouins loved to hold occasional camel races. This tradition is still perpetuated by the royal family in the annual King's Camel Race, staged by the National Guard in the desert near the Riyadh airport. In a creative blend of old and new that is typical of Saudi Arabia today, the Bedouins bring their camels to the racecourse sandwiched into the backs of their Toyota pickup trucks. The race itself is very demanding. It covers about 10 miles (16 km) of desert and takes roughly two hours to complete. The riders can be quite young—boys often do well at this sport—and receive prizes from the King himself if they finish in one of the top five places.

To conserve Saudi Arabia's wildlife, hunting with firearms has been banned since 1977, but falcons are still used to hunt birds, particularly the bustard, a big bird which runs along the ground, and rabbits.

During the hunt itself, the falcon is hooded and perches on the falconer's

THE CAMEL

In the past camels were used by the nomads chiefly to carry their tents and their families from one grazing area to another. An Arabian camel is very hardy and well-adapted to desert life. It does not begin to sweat until its blood temperature has risen considerably.

It does not lose much water when it urinates. If there is enough moisture in the herbs and grass it eats, usually in the winter, a camel can go for one week without additional water. During the summer, however, when the sun is hotter and the grazing dry, it needs to drink every two or three days.

Female camels are the best for nomadic life. They produce a nutritious milk, which the Bedouins drink, for almost half a year after giving birth. They are more docile than male camels and can therefore be used for riding. Furthermore they have more endurance than the males. For all these reasons, female camels are preferred. Male camels are generally killed for their meat when they are still young. The older males are used to carry the tents and other camping gear.

forearm, which is protected from the bird's talons by a heavy leather glove. When the prey is seen, the falcon is unhooded and sent aloft. With its keen eyesight, it quickly spots and attacks the prey, diving at it with sharp talons fully extended. The falcon stays with its catch until the keeper arrives. He rewards it with a tiny bit of meat and then hoods it again. Falcons live up to fifteen years, but they are at their best as hunters during the first five years.

MODERN SPORTS

Getting and staying in good physical shape is not a national preoccupation in Saudi Arabia. The dry heat in the interior of the country and the high humidity along the coasts make outdoor activity something that most Saudis try to avoid during the day. Even those who like to engage in sports find the going difficult. During the heat of the day it is nearly impossible to play exhausting games such as soccer.

Moreover, in the extreme dryness, it is very hard to keep any kind of playing field green enough for even early morning or evening games. However, recently the Kingdom has mastered the art of keeping golf courses green. There are at least six grass courses in addition to several desert courses in the Kingdom.

Despite these limitations there is growing interest in both individual and team sports, especially among Saudi students. Through its Organization for Youth Welfare, the Saudi government has demonstrated its commitment to introducing modern sports to the Kingdom. Basketball has become popular. Facilities for martial arts have been built. The polished tile floors

Saudi teen boys enjoy jet skis on a hot July day in Jeddah.

The port city of
Jeddah offers
amusements for
Saudis and tourists
alike.

of the Nassariya Gate, a public monument in Riyadh, have proved ideal for roller-skating. Most major cities and universities now have swimming pools, athletic fields, tracks, and other facilities for sports. Even though few Saudis feel completely at home in the water, power boating, sailing, water skiing, and jet skiing have caught on in Jeddah.

Some Saudis also like to participate in the sports enjoyed by many of the Western foreigners in the country. These include tennis, horseback riding, camping and rally driving in the desert, boating, fishing, snorkeling, and scuba diving in the Red Sea.

FOOTBALL (SOCCER)

By far the most popular team sport in Saudi Arabia is football, or what Americans call soccer. (It is not the same as American football.) It is played informally in open spaces in the cities and more formally in big stadiums. Football draws eager crowds and is enthusiastically supported by members of the royal family. The King Fahd International Stadium in Riyadh is built around a soccer field and has a capacity for 80,000 spectators. The national team is called the Falcons and the uniforms are the green of the Saudi flag.

Football was first introduced in the Kingdom in the mid-1920s. Its rise in popularity, however, was slow. As interest picked up, a National Arabian Football Federation was set up to encourage the game and to promote the

WOMEN ATHLETES AND THE OLYMPICS

Until 2012, Saudi Arabia barred its women athletes from participating in the Olympic Games. It wasn't a very difficult ban to enforce because, in fact, Saudi Arabia had no women athletes—at least not outwardly. Many conservative Muslims believe that Sharia law forbids women from engaging in such activity. Saudi women and girls who enjoy sports had to practice privately with no social support.

King Abdullah changed this when he made the historic decision to send two teenage girls to the 2012 Games in London—one in judo and one, pictured here, in track and field.

The king made it clear, however, that the young women needed to follow the usual Islamic rules for dress and behavior. While widely applauded internationally, the king's decision was largely made in response to pressure from the International Olympic Committee. The committee had reportedly been considering barring Saudi Arabia from the Olympics until the Kingdom allowed women athletes to compete. Once the king agreed, however, there were no women who even qualified, since Saudi women are quite actively discouraged from playing sports. Nevertheless, the Olympic Committee accepted the two athletes under its "universality" clause. This allows athletes who don't meet qualifying times to compete when their participation is deemed important for reasons of equality.

Following this watershed decision, the Kingdom has reconsidered its stance on allowing girls and women to play sports. It now allows limited physical education for girls in private schools. And in 2013, Saudi Arabia opened its first sports center for girls in the city of Khobar. It offers physical fitness, karate, yoga, and weight loss programs, as well as special activities for children.

official Saudi soccer team. In 1959 Saudi Arabia joined the Federation Internationale de Football Association (FIFA). The Saudis hired foreign soccer coaches to bring their teams up to international standards. Working with these experts, young Saudi players began learning the importance of hard and continued training, punctuality, and self-discipline.

The team's breakthrough in international football came in 1994, when the team qualified for the FIFA World Cup held in the United States. Since then Saudi Arabia has made two more World Cup appearances—in 1998 and 2002. Saudi Arabia has also emerged as the champions in three Asian Cups, and in 2000 mid-fielder Nawaf Al-Temyat was awarded the title of Asian Footballer of the Year.

The Saudi national football team wears the colors of the nation's flag.

INTERNET LINKS

www.iaf.org/HistoryFalconry.php
International Association for Falconry
This site has a section on the history of the sport as well as many other topics.

www.gluckman.com/camelracing.html
"Death in Dubai"
This article, from the early 1990s, offers a glimpse at the dark side of camel racing in Dubai and the UAE, and an update.

photoblog.nbcnews.com/_news/2011/11/11/8742515-robots-replace-children-as-jockeys-in-mideast-camel-racing?lite
A photo essay about camel races using robots instead of jockeys.

FESTIVALS

Young Saudi girls perform at a Spring Festival in Riyadh.

12

S AUDIS CELEBRATE FEWER national holidays and festivals than Westerners do, and they mark them in a different fashion. Rather than having numerous one-day holidays, Saudis have two main special times of the year that extend over a number of days. These religious observations are deeply meaningful and require certain duties, such as fasting. Each of these occasions ends in a festive celebration called an *Eid* (eed).

In addition, there are a few noteworthy days in the year that some Saudis will observe in a special way and others won't. Muharram, for example, is the first month of the Islamic year. Some people will celebrate the first day of Muharram as Islamic New Year.

Within the family there are, of course, joyful occasions—such as the birth of a child or a wedding—that people celebrate with great feasting and merriment, just as they do in most cultures.

THE TWO EIDS

EID AL-FITR The first of the two annual national holidays, *Eid al-Fitr* (eed ahl-FITTER), the Feast of the Breaking of the Fast, is also known as *Eid al-Sagghir* (eed ahl-sahg-HEER), the Little or Lesser Festival. It celebrates the end of the demanding month-long Ramadan daytime fast.

Muslim holidays don't occur on the same day each year. The dates are calculated according to the Islamic, or lunar, calendar and not the Gregorian calendar common to most of the world. A lunar year (based on phases of the moon) has approximately 354 days. Therefore, the observation of Ramadan, for example, moves forward ten or eleven days each year. Sometimes it occurs in the cooler winter months and sometimes in the blazing heat of summer.

The festive sign says, "Happy Eid."

Going without food or drink during the long, hot hours of the desert day from sunrise to sunset is never an easy matter. As a result, the end of the Ramadan fast is a time of happiness and rejoicing.

The exact date of this Eid is never known precisely in advance because it depends on the proper sighting of the moon the night before the festival begins. Sometimes the Eid is announced after midnight, after the children have gone to bed. This makes the celebration a time of suspense for them.

The Eid al-Fitr holiday itself officially lasts three days, when all government and most business offices are closed. In practice, however, much of government and professional life in Saudi Arabia gradually slows down to a near-halt as Eid al-Fitr approaches. This pronounced pause in official and business activity usually lasts about three weeks—one week before the celebration, one week for the holiday itself, and one week after Eid al-Fitr.

Eid al-Fitr is a religious event, but at the same time it is very much a family holiday, in some ways like Thanksgiving in the United States, or Christmas. Although Saudi Arabia is now changing rapidly, and each family may not follow the same customs, the traditional way of celebrating Eid al-Fitr is still observed by many Saudis.

These families get up early and gather together for a quick snack of dates and coffee. This is the first daytime meal taken since the Ramadan fast began. Then it is time for prayers when families go to the mosque. Because of the big crowds celebrating this holiday, Eid prayers are offered not only at small neighborhood mosques but also in very large mosques or on specially consecrated grounds.

After prayers, family members welcome the end of the long fast by greeting one another and their neighbors with the salutation, "Happy Eid!" Then Saudi families enjoy a special big breakfast.

Children love Eid al-Fitr. They not only get new clothes but also presents of candy and money. Both the children and their parents look forward to a traditional sweet, pink, apricot drink with which they break the Ramadan fast.

After breakfast families go visiting from house to house, the younger married members of the family calling on the homes of the elder members. A sheep is slaughtered and cooked for a big lunch hosted by the senior member of the family. In recent years, some amusement parks have opened in Saudi cities and parents often take their young children there during the Eid holidays.

EID AL-ADHA The other Eid is *Eid al-Adha* (eed ahl-AHD-ha, the Feast of the Sacrifice), also known as *Eid al-Kabir* (eed ahl-kah-BEER), the Big Festival. It celebrates the end of the hajj and commemorates Abraham's submission to God, a submission dramatically shown by Abraham's willingness to sacrifice to God his own son, Ishmael.

This Eid is also a joyful time because Muslims feel a profound sense of thanksgiving and accomplishment when they have participated in the hajj. Although the pace of life slows down for Eid al-Adha, this four-day holiday is not celebrated with quite the same sense of excitement as Eid al-Fitr.

However, it also centers on the extended family. A lamb is slaughtered, a big family meal is prepared, and food or alms are given to the poor.

THE PROPHET'S BIRTHDAY

Some people celebrate Mawlid al-Nabi, the birthday of the Prophet Muhammad, and some do not. In fact, Muslims disagree about whether it's proper to celebrate his birthday, or indeed, if such as celebration is actually prohibited. The Prophet's birthday and birthday celebrations in general are not mentioned or called for in the Qu'ran. Therefore many Muslims believe a birthday celebration to be a later-day innovation that is not part of Islam. Others think Muhammad's birthday is a good occasion to rededicate one's self to his teachings. While the exact day is not known with certainty, the Prophet's birthday is usually noted on the twelfth day of Rabi Al-Awwal, the third month of the Islamic calendar. Many predominately Muslim countries mark it as a national holiday, but Saudi Arabia does not.

Saudi girls wave flags during celebrations marking Saudi Arabian National Day in 2013.

SAUDI NATIONAL DAY

One other day that is commemorated officially, the Saudi National Day, marks the unification of the Kingdom of Saudi Arabia in 1932. This national holiday always falls on September 23. It is the only official holiday that is not observed according to the Islamic calendar. The Saudi National Day commemorates the uniting of the country under the name of Saudi Arabia. Technically this is not a holiday because there are no parades or other public events, and people are still expected to go to work.

JENADRIYAH

A popular cultural festival takes place each year in Saudi Arabia. The Jenadriyah is a two-week long celebration of Saudi heritage held in a town of the same name about 30 miles (48 km) northeast of Riyadh.

Families arrive at the Jenadriyah Festival of Heritage and Culture in 2013.

Traditional artisans, craftsmen, and artists showcase their skills alongside exhibitions by major Saudi corporations displaying their latest innovations. Camel and horse races are a big attraction, and there are always lots of tasty Saudi delicacies to enjoy. Musicians play traditional music, and folk dancers entertain the many visitors who attend the festival each year.

In keeping with the Saudi way of doing things, some days and times, the festival is open to men only; other times are for students only; and still other times it is open to families only.

INTERNET LINKS

www.saudiembassy.net/about/country-information/culture_art/jenadrivah_heritage.aspx
The Royal Embassy of Saudi Arabia in Washington, D.C.
This all-purpose site features a short page about the festival

http://sauditourism.sa/en/Events/Pages/HeritageEvent.aspx
The Saudi Tourism site has a long list of festivals and happenings around the country.

FOOD

A mountain of sticky Medjool dates offers a tempting taste of Saudi sweetness.

13

FROM THE SWEET CHEWINESS OF dates to the creamy coolness of yogurt, the warmth of spice, the zing of garlic, the crunch of cucumbers, and the rich meatiness of lamb, Arabian cooking is a festival of flavors and textures. Saudis like to eat well. Whether they are sitting on chairs and eating Western-style food with knife and fork, or squatting on the floor eating a traditional feast of lamb and rice with their fingers, the big serving table is well covered with delicious foods.

Arabs have a strong tradition of hospitality. At a meal, offering several different kinds of food in large quantities is considered good manners. So is setting the table nicely, if possible with elegant silver utensils, and decorating it with bowls of fresh fruit. Saudis love to eat fresh fruit. Grapes, oranges, figs, dates, melons, cherries, and apricots are a common sight on a Saudi table. This lavish hospitality shows the generosity of the host and hostess and their concern for the welfare of their family or guests. Having lots of food in large portions is also a way Saudis show that they honor their guests.

One type of food and a type of beverage are strictly forbidden to Saudis: pork, because it comes from pigs, which are considered unclean by Muslims; and alcohol, which Muslims are not supposed to

The date palm tree not only produces a favorite fruit, it is the national symbol of Saudi Arabia and appears on its flag.

drink. The prohibition for eating pork or drinking alcohol is stated in the Qur'an.

Since Muslims are not permitted to consume alcohol, vegetable and fruit juices are popular alternatives. All sorts of fruit and vegetables are used to make juices that are healthy as well as thirst-quenching. Fruit and vegetable concentrates are also readily available in cans and bottles.

TYPICAL MEALS

Saudis who have been educated in or who have traveled to the West may prefer to sit on chairs at a table when having a meal and to use knives, forks, and spoons. However, the traditional way to eat in Saudi Arabia is to sit on rugs and to use one's right hand to eat. The left hand is considered unclean for eating.

Shoppers pick through sweets and dates at a bazaar in Medina.

Saudis serve both Middle Eastern and Western food, often at the same meal. And since many Saudis of the middle class or of a higher status have domestic helpers—at the minimum, a male cook (usually an Egyptian, Sudanese, or Yemeni)—they do not have to worry about cooking and cleaning up. The modern kitchens in the homes of these Saudis are very similar to the modern kitchens in the United States.

Typical Saudi dishes include *shikamba* (shi-KAHM-bah), a creamy lamb meatball soup; a fruit and vegetable salad made with apples, dates, walnuts, lettuce, mayonnaise, yogurt, and lemon juice; spinach and meat *kofta* (KOOF-tah), spinach, ground lamb or beef, rice, spices, tomato paste, and onion; and onions stuffed with meat and rice. Saudi cooking is usually flavored with many spices, such as cumin, coriander, and cinnamon.

Most Saudis like to end their meals with a sweet dessert, such as *halva* (HAHL-wah), a pasty sweet made from semolina or rice flour and filled with dried apricots, dates, or chopped nuts.

Saudi drinks include raisin tea, made with water in which raisins have been soaked; lemonade; "Saudi champagne," a nonalcoholic carbonated fruit drink; and Arab coffee flavored with cardamon.

A Western-style meal at a Saudi home would be very familiar to Americans. It might include lentil soup, a fish dish, steak, rice, salad, and dessert. Fruit juice and Arab or instant coffee would be served.

Kabsa is a favorite dish of rice and chicken or lamb, often topped with nuts and dried fruits.

SAUDI FEASTS

When feasts are held in the Kingdom today, the traditions of the desert remain popular. The main dish to be served is still very likely to be lamb and spiced rice. This dish is prepared in the traditional way and is known in Arabic as *kabsa* (KAHB-sah). Whole sheep are stewed in giant pots or are roasted. When done, pieces of meat are piled on huge serving platters and surrounded by mounds of spiced rice. The platters are sometimes so big and heavy that two people are needed to carry them to the dozen guests, who sit cross-legged on cushions or rugs in the dining room. Juice from the meat mixes with the melted butter on the hot rice to form a rich, delicious combination.

Side dishes might include eggplant, eggs and cheese, and round flat bread called *khubz* (HOH-boz), which was traditionally used to scoop up food. Fruit or a sweet custard may be served for dessert. Since wine, beer, or any other alcoholic drinks are forbidden, fruit juices may be offered instead.

Guests eat with the fingers of their right hand. When the meal is over, they rinse their fingers in bowls of water, which are sometimes scented

Women attend an all-female banquet in a private home where they can remove their veils.

with roses, brought to them by servants. Tea and Arab coffee end the feast. Shortly after the meal, guests take their leave. It is not the custom, as it is in the West, to linger and chat for a long time after dinner.

The Eid al-Fitr feast is a special event. When night falls on the last day of Ramadan, families break their month-long daylight fast with a wonderful dinner that can last far into the night. Special feast foods include a traditional soup full of wheat, meat, and vegetables; fried pastries stuffed with meat, pine nuts, or cheese; a lemony salad; a lentil dish; yogurt and chickpeas; and eggs fried with ground meat, onions, and tomatoes.

THE COFFEE AND TEA RITUAL

In Saudi Arabia coffee plays an important role as a social lubricant. To this extent, it takes the place that alcohol occupies in other countries. Coffee is served to guests as soon as they arrive. Men meet at the local coffee shop to discuss the day's events. Feasts end immediately after coffee has been served. Because it stimulates people physically and socially, coffee has been used for a long time in the Arabian Peninsula. In fact, some believe that coffee originated here, near Mocha in Yemen, where fine coffee is still grown.

There is a special way to prepare coffee in Saudi Arabia. A small handful of green coffee beans are roasted over a fire. With a pestle, the beans are then pounded in a brass mortar and flavored with cardamom seeds. Water is then added. The coffee is brought to a boil three times, each time in a different brass pot, and is finally poured out by a servant in a long arching stream into tiny cups. The cups are filled only halfway. The custom is never to accept more than three cups; holding out the cup to the server and tilting it from side to side is the sign that you have had enough, and that the server should take away your empty cup.

Saudi men converse over coffee prepared and served in the traditional way.

Small cups of heavily sweetened tea are often offered to visitors as well. There is no special technique involved in brewing tea, but the same basic rule applies: drinking more than three cups is considered bad manners.

SHAWARMA AND OTHER FAST FOODS

Shawarma (shah-WAHR-mah) is a delicious Middle Eastern fast food sold in the souq and elsewhere in cities and towns in Saudi Arabia. It consists of slivers of roasted lamb carved from a spit, which is slowly rotated in front of a hot grill so that the meat is equally browned all over. Making a pocket of flat Arabic bread, the seller adds parsley, lemon juice, tomatoes, and spices and presents the shawarma to you with a smile.

In addition to this traditional snack, Western fast food is also available. It is popular in Saudi Arabia for the same reasons it is elsewhere—it is quick, filling, and cheap.

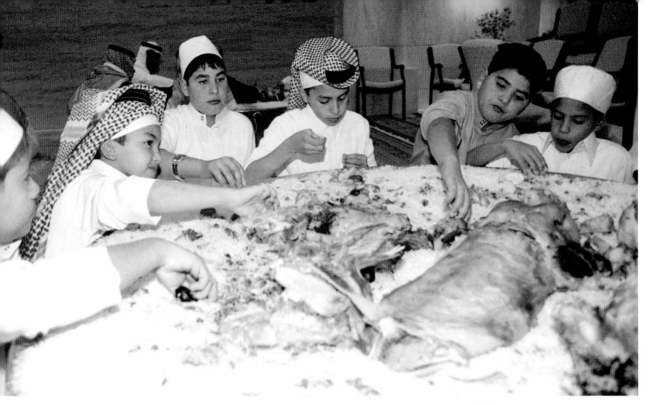

At an Eid al-Fitr celebration, Saudi boys dig in to a huge platter of the traditional dish, stuffed lamb with spiced saffron rice.

ETIQUETTE AND TABLE MANNERS

Genuine friendships based on mutual trust and appreciation are extremely important in Saudi Arabia. They open bureaucratic doors that would otherwise stay closed.

When a Saudi wants to entertain a foreign businessman, he will often invite him for lunch at home. Members of the extended family, on the other hand, are frequently entertained at home in the evening.

A male guest will be introduced to a Saudi's sons and to his young daughters, but he will neither see nor meet his wife or any older daughters. It is considered improper for a man to inquire about another man's wife. Thus the innocent American question, "How's your wife?" would not be well received in the Kingdom. Instead guests may appropriately ask how the sons or young daughters are.

Saudis do not like to call strangers by their first name until they know each other very well and have become friends. A Saudi man who is old and venerable or a young man from a good family may be accorded the honorary title of *sheikh*. If so, he will be addressed by it. An example is Sheikh Yamani.

Otherwise, a man will be addressed as *Sayed* (sah-EED), or Mr.; a married woman is referred to as *Sayedah* (sah-eed-DAH), or Mrs.

At meals there are three main taboos. Since the left hand is considered unclean, only the right hand may be used for eating or for passing food or drink. The soles of the feet are also considered unclean; it is offensive to point them at another person. At a traditional meal where there are no chairs and guests must sit on the floor, they should squat or sit so the bottoms of their feet do not face another person. And, finally, it is impolite to stare at other people while they are eating. Looking down at your own plate instead is considered good manners.

Eating a greasy dish like mutton (lamb) and rice with fingers takes practice and, for one not used to it, is difficult to do gracefully. It is extremely important to use only the fingers of the right hand. The best, and in fact the only, technique for eating politely with fingers is to make a small, compact ball of rice and small pieces of meat, using the fingers and thumb of the right hand. This little ball of rice and meat is then deftly popped into the mouth with the thumb.

INTERNET LINKS

www.al-bab.com/arab/food.htm
Al-Bab: Food in the Arab World
A page with many links to recipes and other food sites.

sauditourism.sa/en/Explore/ThingsToDo/Pages/a-Dishes.aspx
Saudi Tourism presents lists of Saudi traditional foods according to province. There are no recipes, but the names and detailed descriptions give enough information to find a recipe elsewhere online.

www.sookandcook.com
Sook & Cook
A web site for Middle Eastern, Arabic, and Mediterranean food lovers.

SHAKSHUKA

This dish is popular all over the Middle East, where it is often eaten for breakfast. Some variations are saucier, and some recipes call for poaching the eggs in the tomato sauce, rather than scrambling them.

2 tablespoons olive oil or butter
4 medium tomatoes, diced, or one
   28-ounce can of diced tomatoes
2 garlic cloves, minced
1 small white onion, minced
1 small serrano or jalapeño pepper,
   finely chopped (optional)
½ teaspoon salt
½ teaspoon black pepper
1 teaspoon cumin
6 eggs
Fresh cilantro or parsley, coarsely
chopped (optional)

Directions
Heat oil in a medium sauté pan over a medium heat. Add onions, peppers, and garlic until tender, about 2—3 minutes. Add tomatoes, salt, pepper, and cumin and stir well. Cook 2—4 minutes until tomatoes soften.

In a medium size bowl, lightly beat eggs with a fork. Pour eggs over mixture and let set over medium-low heat, stirring lightly a few times, for another 3—5 minutes or until done. Alternatively, poach whole eggs in tomato sauce and let set over medium low heat until cooked to taste. Sprinkle with cilantro or parsley. Serve with warm flat bread.

SAUDI ARABIAN DATE BALLS

¼—⅓ cup all-purpose flour
1 ½ cups soft dates, pitted and chopped
4 Tablespoons unsalted butter
½ teaspoon cardamom, ground
½ cup walnuts, chopped
1 Tablespoon brown sugar
Granulated sugar or flaked coconut (optional)

Directions
Chop dates and walnuts. If you are using a food processor, start with the walnuts. Chop into small bits, not too chunky and not too fine. Remove from the bowl and set aside; then chop the dates. If starting with whole dates, be sure to first remove the pits. Sprinkle the dates with a little granulated sugar to keep the blade from sticking. Chop into smallish bits. Melt butter in a medium-sized skillet over medium heat. Add walnuts and mix until lightly toasted. Add cardamom, brown sugar, dates, and flour. Mix until nuts and dates are covered. Remove from heat.

Cover your hands with plastic bags and shape mixture into walnut-size ball shapes. Roll balls in granulated sugar or flaked coconut, if desired.

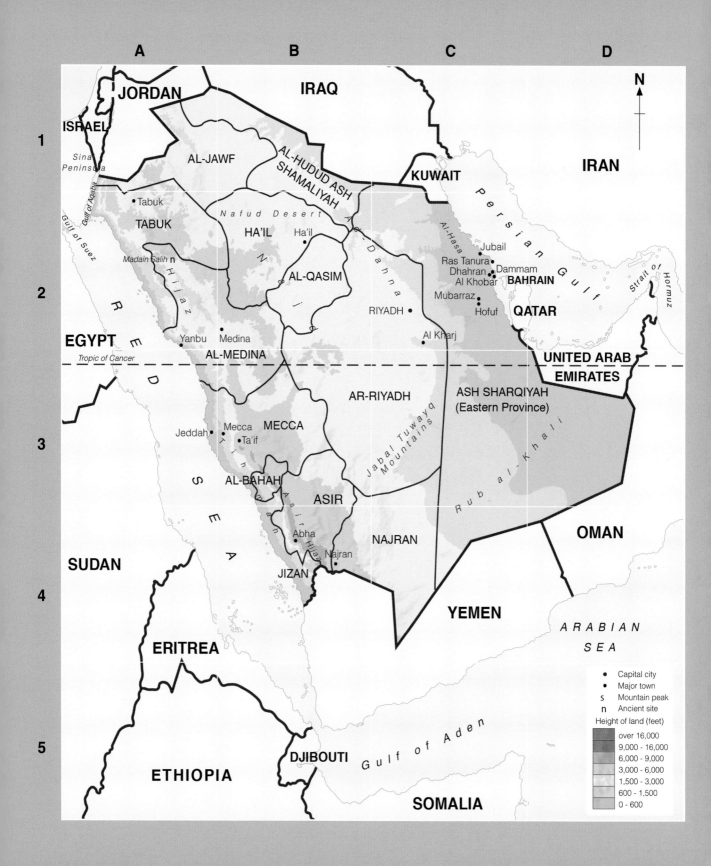

Abha, B4
Ad-Dahna, B2—C2
Al-Bahah, B3
Al-Hasa, C2
Al-Hudud ash Shamaliyah, A1, B1—B2
Al-Jawf, A1—A2, B1—B2
Al Kharj, C2
Al Khobar, C2
Al-Medina, A2—A3, B2—B3
Al-Qasim, B2
Ar-Riyadh, B2—B3, C2—C3
Arabian Sea, D4—D5
Ash Sharqiyah (Eastern province), B2, C2—C4, D3—D4
Asir (province), B3—B4
Asir Mountains, B3—B4

Bahrain, C2

Dammam, C2
Dhahran, C2
Djibouti, B5

Egypt, A2—A3
Eritrea, A4—A5, B4—B5
Ethiopia, A5—B5

Gulf of Aden, B5—C5
Gulf of Aqaba, A1—A2
Gulf of Suez, A2

Ha'il, B2
Ha'il (province), B2
Hijaz (region), A2, B3—B4
Hijaz Mountains, A2—A3
Hofuf, C2

Iran, C1, D1—D2
Iraq, B2—C2
Israel, A1

Jabal Tuwayq Mountains, C3
Jeddah, A3
Jizan (province), B3—B4
Jordan, A1
Jubail, C2

Kuwait, C1—C2

Lebanon, A1

Madain Salih, A2
Mecca, B3
Mecca (province), A3—B3
Medina, B2
Mediterranean Sea, A1

Mubarraz, C2

Nafud Desert, B2Najd (region), B2
Najd (region), B2
Najran, B4
Najran (province), B3—B4, C3—C4

Oman, D2—D4

Persian Gulf, C1—C2, D2

Qatar, C2

Ras Tanura, C2
Red Sea, A2—A4, B3—B5
Riyadh, C2
Rub al-Khali, C3—C4, D3—D4

Sinai Peninsula, A1—A2
Somalia, B5—C5
Strait of Hormuz, D2
Sudan, A3—A5

Tabuk, A2

Tabuk (province), A1—A2, B2
Ta'if, B3
Tihamah, B3—B4

United Arab Emirates, D2—D3

Yanbu, A2
Yemen, B4—B5, C4—C5, D4

133

ECONOMIC SAUDI ARABIA

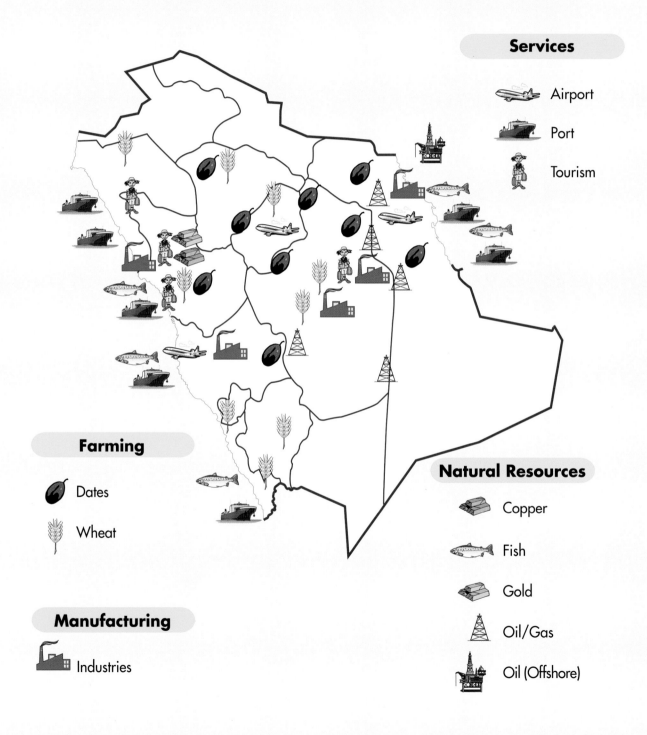

Services

Airport

Port

Tourism

Farming

Dates

Wheat

Manufacturing

Industries

Natural Resources

Copper

Fish

Gold

Oil/Gas

Oil (Offshore)

ABOUT THE ECONOMY

OVERVIEW

Saudi Arabia has an oil-based economy. It has the largest petroleum reserves in the world and is the largest exporter of petroleum. Saudi Arabia plays a leading role in OPEC. The government is encouraging private-sector growth to lessen the country's reliance on the petroleum industry and to employ more Saudi citizens. More than five million foreign workers play an important role in the Saudi economy, particularly in the oil and service sectors. Meanwhile, the country struggles with unemployment among its own citizens.

GROSS DOMESTIC PRODUCT (GDP)

$883.7 billion (2012)

CURRENCY

1 US dollar = 3.75 Saudi Arabia Riyal (SAR) (February 2014)
1 Saudi Arabia Riyal (SAR) = 100 halalah
5 halalah = 20 qurush
Notes: 1, 5, 10, 50, 100, 500 Riyal
Coins: 1, 2, 5, 10 qurush; 5, 10, 25, 50 halalah

LAND AREA

772,204 square miles (2,149,690 square kilometers)

LAND USE

Arable land 1.45 percent, other 98.4 percent (2011)

NATURAL RESOURCES

Petroleum, natural gas, iron ore, gold, copper

AGRICULTURAL PRODUCTS

Wheat, barley, tomatoes, melons, dates, citrus, mutton, chickens, eggs, milk

LABOR FORCE

8 million. Note: about 80 percent of the labor force is non-national (2012).

LABOR FORCE BY OCCUPATION

agriculture: 6.7 percent
industry: 21.4 percent
services: 71.9 (2005)

MAJOR EXPORTS

Petroleum and petroleum products, 90 percent

MAJOR IMPORTS

Machinery and equipment, foodstuffs, chemicals, motor vehicles, textiles

MAJOR TRADE PARTNERS

United States 14.2 percent, China 13.6 percent, Japan 13.6 percent, South Korea 9.9 percent, India 8.2 percent, Singapore 4.3 percent (2012)

MAJOR SEAPORTS

Ad Dammam, Al Jubayl, Jeddah, Yanbu al Bahr

AIRPORTS

214 total; 82 with paved runways (2013)

CULTURAL SAUDI ARABIA

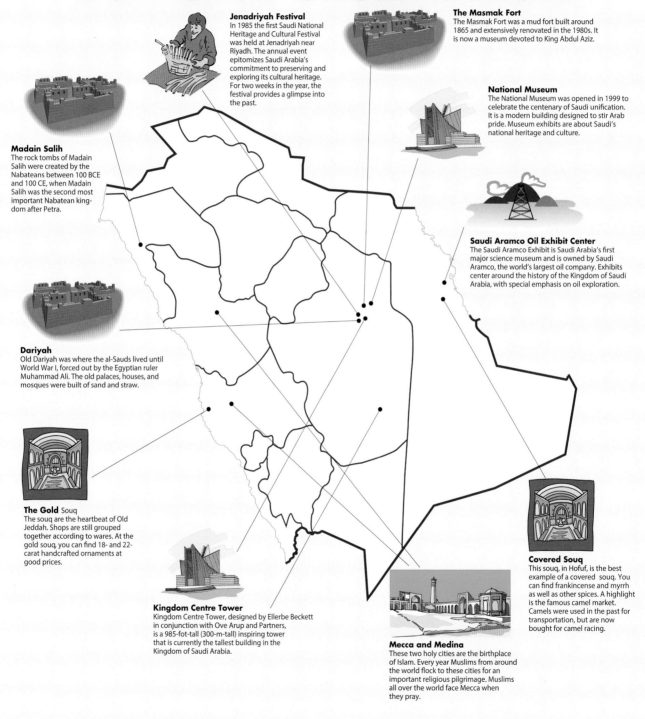

Jenadriyah Festival
In 1985 the first Saudi National Heritage and Cultural Festival was held at Jenadriyah near Riyadh. The annual event epitomizes Saudi Arabia's commitment to preserving and exploring its cultural heritage. For two weeks in the year, the festival provides a glimpse into the past.

The Masmak Fort
The Masmak Fort was a mud fort built around 1865 and extensively renovated in the 1980s. It is now a museum devoted to King Abdul Aziz.

National Museum
The National Museum was opened in 1999 to celebrate the centenary of Saudi unification. It is a modern building designed to stir Arab pride. Museum exhibits are about Saudi's national heritage and culture.

Madain Salih
The rock tombs of Madain Salih were created by the Nabateans between 100 BCE and 100 CE, when Madain Salih was the second most important Nabatean kingdom after Petra.

Saudi Aramco Oil Exhibit Center
The Saudi Aramco Exhibit is Saudi Arabia's first major science museum and is owned by Saudi Aramco, the world's largest oil company. Exhibits center around the history of the Kingdom of Saudi Arabia, with special emphasis on oil exploration.

Dariyah
Old Dariyah was where the al-Sauds lived until World War I, forced out by the Egyptian ruler Muhammad Ali. The old palaces, houses, and mosques were built of sand and straw.

The Gold Souq
The souq are the heartbeat of Old Jeddah. Shops are still grouped together according to wares. At the gold souq, you can find 18- and 22-carat handcrafted ornaments at good prices.

Covered Souq
This souq, in Hofuf, is the best example of a covered souq. You can find frankincense and myrrh as well as other spices. A highlight is the famous camel market. Camels were used in the past for transportation, but are now bought for camel racing.

Kingdom Centre Tower
Kingdom Centre Tower, designed by Ellerbe Beckett in conjunction with Ove Arup and Partners, is a 985-fot-tall (300-m-tall) inspiring tower that is currently the tallest building in the Kingdom of Saudi Arabia.

Mecca and Medina
These two holy cities are the birthplace of Islam. Every year Muslims from around the world flock to these cities for an important religious pilgrimage. Muslims all over the world face Mecca when they pray.

OFFICIAL NAME
The Kingdom of Saudi Arabia

DESCRIPTION OF NATIONAL FLAG
Green with a sword centered horizontally at the base and the inscription in Arabic, "There is no god but God; Muhammad is the Messenger of God."

NATIONAL ANTHEM
Al Salam Al Malaki (Royal Anthem of Saudi Arabia) www.nationalanthems.info/sa.htm

NATIONAL LANGUAGE
Arabic

CAPITAL
Riyadh

GOVERNMENT
Saudi Arabia is governed by a king who serves both as chief of state and head of the government. The present king is Abdullah bin Abd al-Aziz Al Saud, who became king in 2005. His half-brother, Salman bin Abd al-Aziz Al Saud, is the Crown Prince and First Deputy Prime Minister. The cabinet is appointed by the king, and includes many members of the royal family. The king also appoints the members of the 150-member legislative body known as the Consultative Council. There is also a judicial branch, in which judges make decisions based on Islamic Law. There are no national elections or political parties in Saudi Arabia.

PROVINCES
Al-Bahah, Al-Hudud Shamaliya, Al-Jawf, Al-Medina, Al-Qasim, Ar-Riyadh, Ash Sharqiyah (Eastern Province), Asir, Ha'il, Jizan, Mecca, Najran, and Tabuk

POPULATION
26.9 million (2013 est)

LIFE EXPECTANCY
Total population: 74.5 years (2013)
Male: 72.5 years
Female: 76.7 years

LITERACY RATE
87.2 percent

RELIGION
Islam

MAJOR HOLIDAYS
Eid al-Fitr/Eid al-Sagghir (date varies), Eid al-Adha/Eid al-Kabir (date varies), National Day (September 23)

TIMELINE

IN SAUDI ARABIA	IN THE WORLD
	753 BCE Rome is founded.
	116–17 BCE Roman Empire reaches its greatest extent, under Emperor Trajan (98–17).
100 BCE Nabateans begin building Madain Salih.	
106 CE Romans capture the town of Petra to control trade routes. Nabatean civilization begins to decline.	
570 Prophet Muhammad is born in Mecca.	
	600 CE Height of Mayan civilization
610 Year of the Hijrah and the birth of the Islamic calendar	
	1000 Chinese perfect gunpowder and begin to use it in warfare.
1400s Mamluks control the Hijaz region, including the holy cities of Mecca and Medina.	
1517 Ottoman Turks gain control of the Hijaz.	
	1530 Beginning of trans-Atlantic slave trade organized by the Portuguese in Africa
	1558–1603 Reign of Elizabeth I of England
	1620 Pilgrims sail the Mayflower to America.
1750 Muhammad bin Abdul Wahab and Muhammad bin Saud join forces to purify Islam.	
	1776 U.S. Declaration of Independence
	1789–99 French Revolution
1818 Ottoman Turks capture the Saud ancestral home.	
	1861 U.S. Civil War begins.
	1869 Suez Canal is opened.
1891 The powerful Rashid dynasty seizes Riyadh.	
1902 Abdul Aziz Ibn Saud recaptures Riyadh in a fierce battle.	
	1914 World War I begins.

IN SAUDI ARABIA	IN THE WORLD
1932	
Unification of Arab tribes to form the Kingdom of Saudi Arabia	
1938	**1939**
Discovery of oil at Dammam	World War II begins.
1945	**1945**
Saudi Arabia signs the United Nations Charter.	United States drops atomic bombs on Hiroshima and Nagasaki.
	1949
1953	North Atlantic Treaty Organization (NATO) is
King Abdul Aziz dies; his eldest son, Saud, becomes king.	formed.
	1957
1960	Russians launch Sputnik.
Organization of Petroleum-Exporting Countries (OPEC) is formed.	
1964	
King Faisal becomes king when his brother Saud abdicates.	**1966–69**
1981	Chinese Cultural Revolution
Saudi Arabia becomes a founding member of the Gulf Cooperation Council.	**1986**
1990	Nuclear power disaster at Chernobyl in Ukraine
Gulf War—Iraq invades Kuwait.	**1991**
	Break-up of the Soviet Union
1996	**1997**
Khobar Towers housing complex is destroyed by suicide bombers.	Hong Kong is returned to China.
	2001
2005	September 11: Fifteen of the nineteen hijackers involved in attacks on New York and Washington are Saudi nationals.
King Fahd dies. He is succeeded by the former crown prince, Abdullah.	
2013	**2013**
King Abdullah swears in thirty women to the previously all-male Shura consultative council. It is the first time women have been able to hold any political office.	Argentine cleric Jorge Bergoglio becomes Pope Francis I, head of the Roman Catholic Church.
	2014
2015	The Crimea votes to secede from Ukraine and join Russia.
Saudi women to have the right to vote and run for municipal office.	

GLOSSARY

abaya (ah-BAH-yah)
A long black cloak worn by Saudi women.

gutra (GOOT-rah)
A flowing head covering worn by Saudi men.

hadith (hah-DEETH)
A record of wise sayings and traditions originating with Prophet Muhammad.

hajj (HAHJ)
The pilgrimage to Mecca, required of all Muslims who are able to go.

hareem (hah-REEM)
Women's quarters.

Ka 'bah (kah-AH-bah)
Holy monument in the Grand Mosque of Mecca, toward which Muslims pray.

khubz (HOH-boz)
A round, flat Arabic bread.

Kufi (koo-FEE)
Arabic script found in early copies of the Qur'an.

majlis (MAHJ-lis)
A public audience presided over by government officials whereby people can personally present their petitions.

muezzin (moo-EZ-in)
A man who calls Muslims to prayer from a mosque, via loudspeakers.

mutawa (MOO-tah-wah)
Religious police.

Ramadan (rah-mah-DHAN)
The ninth month of the Islamic calendar, a time of fasting and atonement for sins

Sayed (sah-EED)
Title of men; equivalent to "Mr."

Sayedah (sah-eed-DAH)
Title of married women; equivalent of "Mrs."

shahadah (shah-HAH-dah)
Prayer professing faith: "There is no god but God, and Muhammad is His Messenger."

sheikh
A tribal leader, an elder.

souq (SOOK)
A traditional market.

surah (SOO-rah)
A chapter in the Qur'an.

thobe (THOH-bay)
A long white robe worn by Saudi men.

umm (OOM)
The name by which a woman is known when she has a son; literally "mother of."

zakat (ZAH-kaht)
A charitable offering.

FOR FURTHER INFORMATION

BOOKS

Al-Rasheed, Madawi. *History of Saudi Arabia*, second edition. New York: Cambridge University Press, 2010.

Ali-Karamali, Sumbul. *Growing Up Muslim: Understanding the Beliefs and Practices of Islam*. New York: Ember, an imprint of Random House Children's Books, 2013 (Note: This is about growing up Muslim in the United States. This is not a book about Saudi Arabia.)

Aslan, Reza. *No god but God: The Origins and Evolution of Islam*. New York: Ember, an imprint of Random House Children's Books, 2011.

Harik, Ramsay M. and Elsa Marston. *Women in the Middle East: Tradition and Change*. New York: Scholastic Library Publishing, 2003.

Harper, Robert Alexander. *Saudi Arabia*. Pennsylvania: Chelsea House Publishers, 2002.

Mahdi, Ali Akbar. *Teen Life in the Middle East (Teen Life Around the World)*. Westport, Conn.: Greenwood, 2003

Marrin, Albert. *Black Gold: The Story of Oil in Our Lives*. New York: Knopf Books for Young Readers, 2013.

Salloum, Habeeb. *The Arabian Nights Cookbook: From Lamb Kebabs to Baba Ghanouj, Delicious Homestyle Arabian Cooking*. North Clarendon, Vermont: Tuttle Publishing, 2010

WEBSITES

Central Intelligence Agency World Factbook (select Saudi Arabia from the list). www.odci.gov/cia/ publications/factbook/index.html

Lonely Planet World Guides: Destination Saudi Arabia. www.lonelyplanet.com/destinations/middle_east/saudi_arabia

Official website for the Saudi Arabian Oil Company (Saudi Aramco). www.saudiaramco.com

Royal Embassy of Saudi Arabia, Washington D.C. www.saudiembassy.net

Saudi Arabia: A Country Study (select Saudi Arabia). lcweb2.loc.gov/frd/cs/cshome.html

Saudi Arabia's Ministry of Information. www.saudinf.com

Kingdom of Saudi Arabia Ministry of Hajj. www.haj.gov.sa/en-US/Pages/Home.aspx

The World Bank Group (type "Saudi Arabia" in the search box). www.worldbank.org

VIDEOS AND MOVIES

Muhammad: Legacy of a Prophet. DVD. Unity Productions Foundation, 2002

Wadjda. DVD. Sony Pictures Classics, 2012. This award-winning Saudi Arabian-German film, written and directed by Haifaa al-Mansour, is the first feature film shot entirely in Saudi Arabia and is the first feature-length film made by a female Saudi director. It was the first Saudi Arabian movie ever submitted to the Academy Awards for Best Foreign Language.

BIBLIOGRAPHY

BOOKS AND WEBSITES

Al-Rasheed, Madawi. *A History of Saudi Arabia*. New York: Cambridge University Press, 2002.

Country Profile: Saudi Arabia. Library of Congress, 2006.
http://lcweb2.loc.gov/frd/cs/profiles/Saudi_Arabia.pdf

Eakin, Hugh. "Will Saudi Arabia Ever Change?" New York: The New York Review of Books, January 10, 2013.

El-Tahri, Jihan and Martin Smith. "House of Saud." PBS Frontline, WGBH Educational Foundation, 2005. www.pbs.org/wgbh/pages/frontline/shows/saud/

Ingham, Bruce. *Simple Guide to Customs and Etiquette in Saudi Arabia and the Gulf States*. Kent, England: Paul Norbury, 1994.

Leeming, David. *Oxford Companion to World Mythology*. USA: Oxford University Press, 2009.

Mackey, Sandra. *The Saudis: Inside the Desert Kingdom*. Updated edition. New York: W.W. Norton & Company, 2002.

Montagne, Renee, Steve Inskeep, and Yaroslav Trofimov. "1979: Remembering 'The Siege of Mecca.'" NPR, 2009. www.npr.org/templates/story/story.php?storyId=112051155

Royal Embassy of Saudi Arabia, Washington D.C. www.saudiembassy.net

Saudi Arabia Ministry of Information. www.saudinf.com

Saudi Arabia Profile, BBC News, 2013. www.bbc.co.uk/news/world-middle-east-14702705

World Factbook. Middle East: Saudi Arabia. Central Intelligence Agency, 2014. www.odci.gov/cia/publications/factbook/index.html

INDEX

INDEX